PUBLISHING

No nonsense Number Fractions

Ages 8–10 **Book 2**

Jackie Andrews • Jude Callaghan • Suzi de Gouveia

Title: No Nonsense Number Fractions Ages 8-10 Book 2

Authors: Suzi de Gouveia, Jackie Andrews and Jude Callaghan

Editor: Tanya Tremewan

Book Code: PB00087

ISBN: 978-1-908735-67-6

Published: 2012

Publisher: TTS Group Ltd

Park Lane Business Park
Kirkby-in-Ashfield
Notts, NG17 9GU
Tel: 0800 318 686
Fax: 0800 137 525

Website: www.tts-shopping.com

About the authors: Suzi is the enthusiastic principal of St Teresa's Primary School in Christchurch, New Zealand. She has international teaching experience and has had the pleasure of teaching in a multi-cultural environment. Over 20 years of teaching have enabled Suzi to develop a wealth of ideas and resources to best help children.

Jackie is an experienced teacher who has taught middle primary children in both New Zealand and the United Kingdom. As a mother of three young children she is taking time out of the classroom and is enjoying having the time to diversify.

Jude is an experienced, enthusiastic teacher with a passion for teaching and learning. Her teaching programmes are innovative and exciting. Jude has embraced the Numeracy Development Programme wholeheartedly. She has joined the No Nonsense Number writing team to share her deep understanding and wealth of ideas.

Contents

Introduction

This book is targeted at pupils who are working in Years 4–5 and includes child-friendly learning activities to encourage the development of these concepts.

This book contains two sections. The first section comprises of activity sheets to support the learning and consolidation of the concept of fractions.

The second section is comprised of activity cards. These templates can be used in a variety of ways to develop fraction knowledge through independent, individual and group work.

Answers have been provided where appropriate. In some cases, model answers represent only one possibility; one or more variations may also be correct.

Curriculum links (Years 4–5)

Core learning in mathematics: objectives *Most children learn to:*
Year 4 *Counting and understanding number*: Recognise and continue number sequences formed by counting on or back in steps of constant size Use decimal notation for tenths and hundredths Use diagrams to identify equivalent fractions *Calculating*: Find fractions of numbers, quantities or shapes
Year 5 *Counting and understanding number:* Explain what each digit represents in decimals with up to two places, and round these numbers *Calculating:* Find fractions using division

Source: Adapted from the Primary Framework for Literacy and Mathematics 2006

Working with fraction symbols and names

I am learning fraction symbols and names.

Cut out each rocket part. Then make each rocket by matching up all the parts in the rocket family. Stick each rocket in your book.

I am learning the symbols for common fractions.

A. What fraction of these ice creams has been shaded in each box? Match the symbol to the fraction shown.

1.

2.

3.

$\frac{2}{3}$ $\frac{3}{4}$ $\frac{2}{5}$ $\frac{4}{5}$ $\frac{3}{4}$ $\frac{2}{3}$

4.

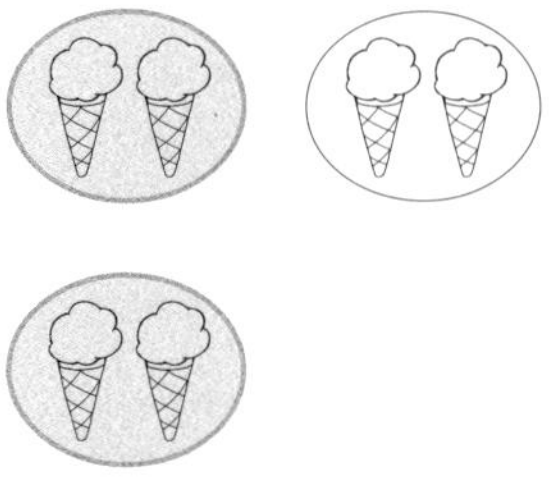

5.

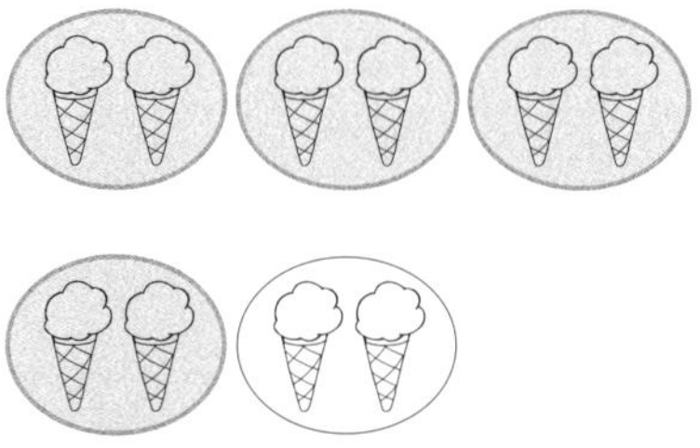

6.

B. Draw your own pictures to show these fractions.

1. $\frac{2}{3}$ of a set

3. $\frac{2}{5}$ of a set

2. $\frac{3}{4}$ of a set

4. $\frac{3}{5}$ of a set

Using equal sharing to find a fraction

I am learning to find a fraction of a number of objects by equal sharing ($\frac{1}{3}$, $\frac{1}{5}$, $\frac{1}{8}$).

Solve these word problems.

A. Judy had a bag of sweets. She gave $\frac{1}{3}$ of them to Peter and $\frac{1}{3}$ of them to Rob. She gave **2** sweets to Mum. There were **7** sweets left in the bag.

1. How many sweets did Peter get? ______
2. How many sweets did Judy start with? ______

B. Chris had a huge bunch of flowers. He gave $\frac{1}{5}$ to Jackie and $\frac{2}{5}$ to Sarah. He gave **4** flowers to Caitlin and he had **10** left in his bunch.

1. How many flowers did Jackie get? ______
2. How many flowers did Sarah get? ______
3. How many flowers did Chris start with? ______

C. Suzi loved her gold bracelets. She had $\frac{2}{10}$ of her collection in her jewellery box. Kristy had borrowed $\frac{3}{10}$ and Gabi had borrowed $\frac{2}{10}$. Suzi was wearing 12 bracelets.

1. How many bracelets were in the jewellery box? ______
2. How many did Suzi have altogether? ______

D. Ben bought some new fish for his tank. $\frac{1}{4}$ of the new fish were guppies, $\frac{1}{8}$ were neons and the remaining 10 were clown loaches.

1. How many new fish were guppies? ______
2. How many new fish did Ben buy altogether? ______

Introducing fractions greater than one

I am learning to identify fractions greater than one.

Each alien has written the fraction on its tummy in the wrong way. Help it find its ship with the fraction written correctly. Draw a line to the ship.

I am learning to identify fractions greater than one.

Complete the table. The first row is done for you.

1.		$\frac{5}{4}$	$1\frac{1}{4}$
2.		$\frac{9}{2}$	
3.			$1\frac{4}{5}$
4.	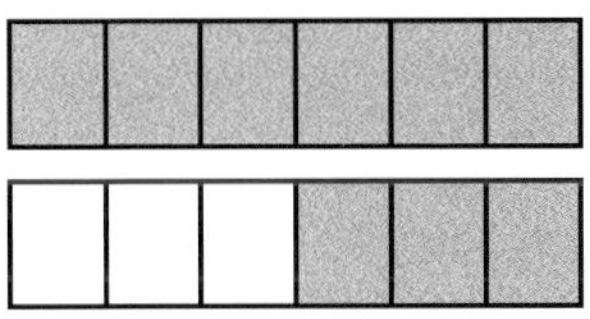		
5.		$\frac{9}{3}$	
6.			$1\frac{3}{4}$
7.	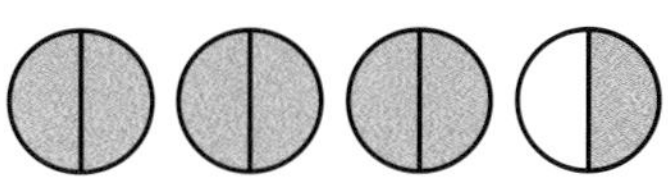		
8.			$2\frac{1}{2}$
9.		$\frac{6}{5}$	
10.			

Working on strategies to find fractions of a set

I am learning to find a fraction of a set using doubles.

Complete these problems. The first one is started for you.

1.

4 + 4 = 8

$\frac{1}{2}$ of 8 = ____

2.

9 + 9 = ____

$\frac{1}{2}$ of ____ = ____

3.

7 + 7 = ____

$\frac{1}{2}$ of ____ = ____

4.

10 + 10 = ____

$\frac{1}{2}$ of ____ = ____

5.

2 + 2 = ____

$\frac{1}{2}$ of ____ = ____

6.

6 + 6 = ____

$\frac{1}{2}$ of ____ = ____

7.

11 + 11 = ____

$\frac{1}{2}$ of ____ = ____

8.

3 + 3 = ____

$\frac{1}{2}$ of ____ = ____

9.

5 + 5 = ____

$\frac{1}{2}$ of ____ = ____

10.

8 + 8 = ____

$\frac{1}{2}$ of ____ = ____

I am learning to find a fraction of a set using addition facts.

Complete these problems.

1.

____ + ____ + ____ = ____

$\frac{1}{3}$ of 9 = ____

2.

____ + ____ + ____ = ____

$\frac{1}{3}$ of 12 = ____

3.

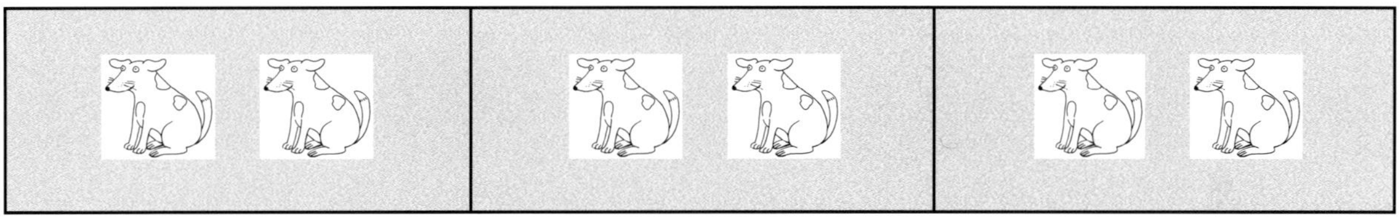

____ + ____ + ____ = ____

$\frac{1}{3}$ of 6 = ____

4.

____ + ____ + ____ = ____

$\frac{1}{3}$ of 15 = ____

5.

____ + ____ + ____ = ____

$\frac{2}{3}$ of 12 = ____

I am learning to find a fraction of a set using addition facts.

Complete these problems.

1.

____ + ____ + ____ + ____ = ____

$\frac{1}{4}$ of 8 = ____

2.

____ + ____ + ____ + ____ = ____

$\frac{1}{4}$ of 16 = ____

3.

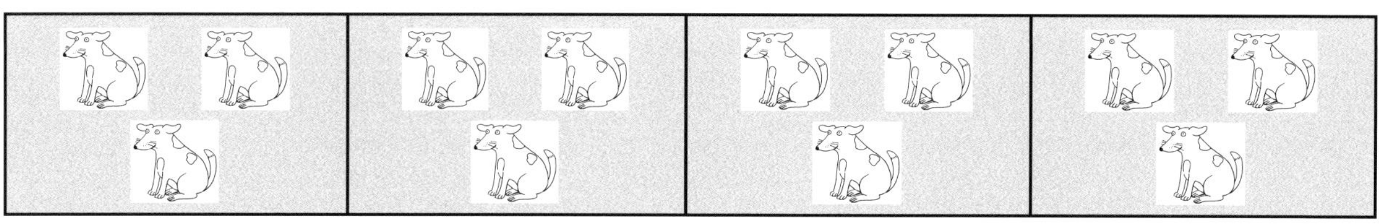

____ + ____ + ____ + ____ = ____

$\frac{1}{4}$ of 12 = ____

4.

____ + ____ + ____ + ____ = ____

$\frac{3}{4}$ of 16 = ____

5.

____ + ____ + ____ + ____ = ____

$\frac{3}{4}$ of 8 = ____

I am learning to find a fraction of a set using addition facts.

Complete these problems.

1. 6 + 6 + 6 = ____

$\frac{1}{3}$ of ____ = ____

5. 5 + 5 + 5 + 5 + 5 = ____

$\frac{1}{5}$ of ____ = ____

2. 9 + 9 + 9 + 9 = ____

$\frac{1}{4}$ of ____ = ____

6. 12 + 12 + 12 = ____

$\frac{1}{3}$ of ____ = ____

3. 10 + 10 + 10 = ____

$\frac{1}{3}$ of ____ = ____

7. 100 + 100 + 100 + 100 = ____

$\frac{1}{4}$ of ____ = ____

4. 6 + 6 + 6 + 6 + 6 = ____

$\frac{1}{5}$ of ____ = ____

8. 20 + 20 + 20 + 20 = ____

$\frac{1}{4}$ of ____ = ____

9. 8 + 8 + 8 + 8 + 8 + 8 + 8 + 8 + 8 + 8 = ____

$\frac{1}{10}$ of ____ = ____

10. 50 + 50 + 50 + 50 + 50 + 50 + 50 + 50 = ____

$\frac{1}{8}$ of ____ = ____

11. 2 + 2 + 2 + 2 + 2 + 2 + 2 + 2 = ____

$\frac{1}{8}$ of ____ = ____

12. 3 + 3 + 3 + 3 + 3 + 3 + 3 + 3 + 3 + 3 = ____

$\frac{1}{10}$ of ____ = ____

I am learning to find fractions of a set using addition facts.

Use your addition facts to find the answers for each set of leaves.

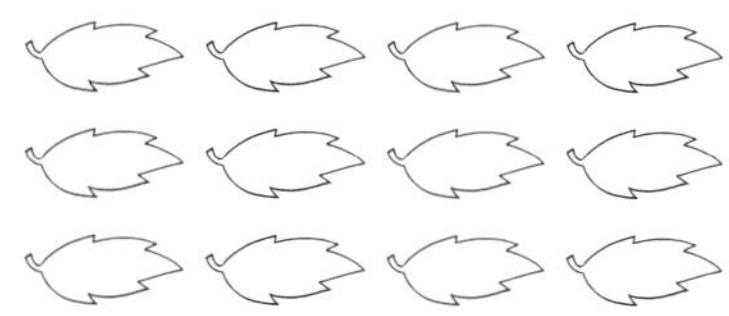

1. $\frac{1}{3}$ of 12 = ____
2. $\frac{2}{3}$ of 12 = 4 + 4 = ____
3. $\frac{3}{3}$ of 12 = 4 + ____ + ____ = ____

4. $\frac{1}{3}$ of 15 = ____
5. $\frac{2}{3}$ of 15 = ____ + ____ = ____
6. $\frac{3}{3}$ of 15 = ____ + ____ + ____ = ____

7. $\frac{1}{4}$ of 16 = ____
8. $\frac{2}{4}$ of 16 = ____ + ____ = ____
9. $\frac{3}{4}$ of 16 = ____ + ____ + ____ = ____
10. $\frac{4}{4}$ of 16 = ____ + ____ + ____ + ____ = ____

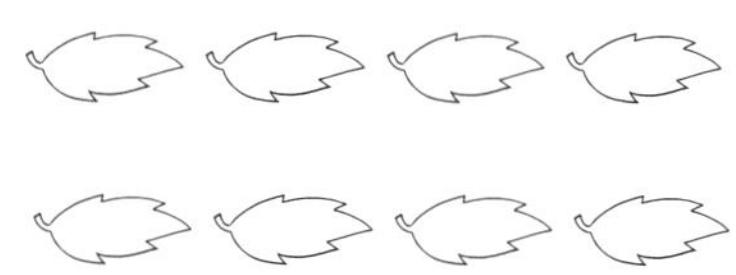

11. $\frac{1}{4}$ of 8 = ____
12. $\frac{2}{4}$ of 8 = ____ + ____ = ____
13. $\frac{3}{4}$ of 8 = ____ + ____ + ____ = ____
14. $\frac{4}{4}$ of 8 = ____ + ____ + ____ + ____ = ____

15. $\frac{1}{4}$ of 12 = ____
16. $\frac{2}{4}$ of 12 = ____ + ____ = ____
17. $\frac{3}{4}$ of 12 = ____ + ____ + ____ = ____
18. $\frac{4}{4}$ of 12 = ____ + ____ + ____ + ____ = ____

19. $\frac{1}{5}$ of 20 = ____
20. $\frac{2}{5}$ of 20 = ____ + ____ = ____
21. $\frac{3}{5}$ of 20 = ____ + ____ + ____ = ____
22. $\frac{4}{5}$ of 20 = ____ + ____ + ____ + ____ = ____
23. $\frac{5}{5}$ of 20 = ____ + ____ + ____ + ____ + ____ = ____

I am learning to find a fraction of a set of objects using addition facts.

Use addition facts to solve the problems.

1.	$\frac{2}{3}$ of 15	
2.	$\frac{3}{5}$ of 35	
3.	$\frac{3}{10}$ of 30	
4.	$\frac{3}{4}$ of 24	
5.	$\frac{4}{5}$ of 50	
6.	$\frac{3}{8}$ of 32	
7.	$\frac{9}{10}$ of 40	
8.	$\frac{2}{4}$ of 48	
9.	$\frac{7}{10}$ of 100	
10.	$\frac{5}{8}$ of 64	

Finding fractions of shapes lengths

I am learning to find fractions of a shape and length.

1. Colour $\frac{1}{4}$ red.
   Colour $\frac{1}{2}$ yellow.

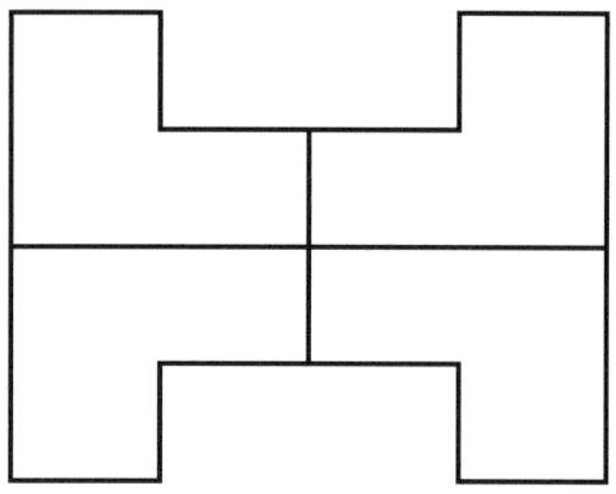

2. Colour $\frac{3}{8}$ orange.
   Colour $\frac{1}{8}$ red.
   Colour $\frac{1}{2}$ blue.

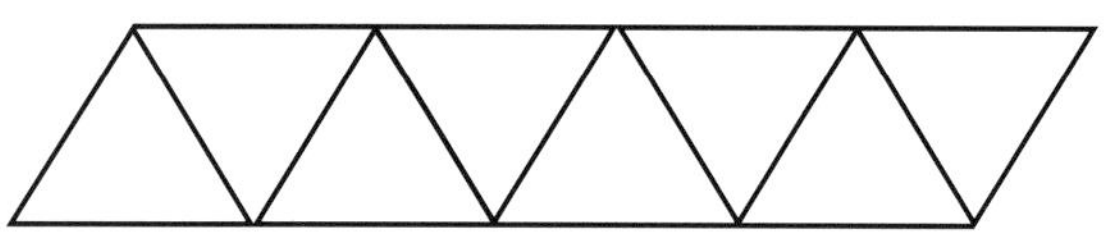

3. Colour $\frac{4}{5}$ red.
   Colour $\frac{2}{10}$ blue.

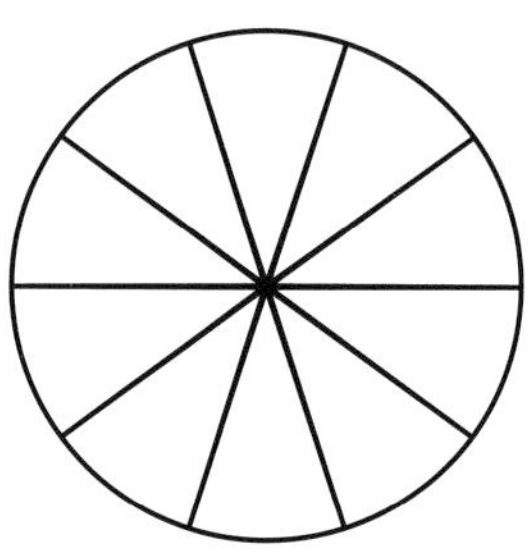

4. Divide this shape into fifths.

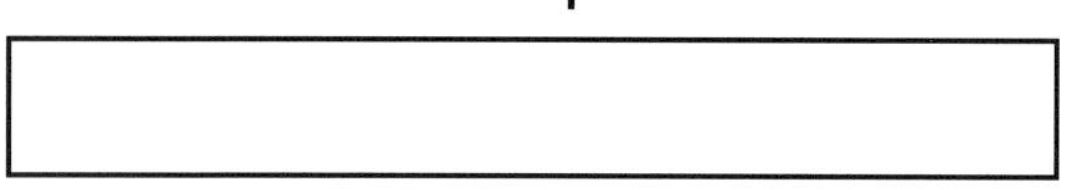

5. Divide this shape into tenths.

6. Colour $\frac{2}{5}$ red.
   Colour $\frac{3}{5}$ yellow.

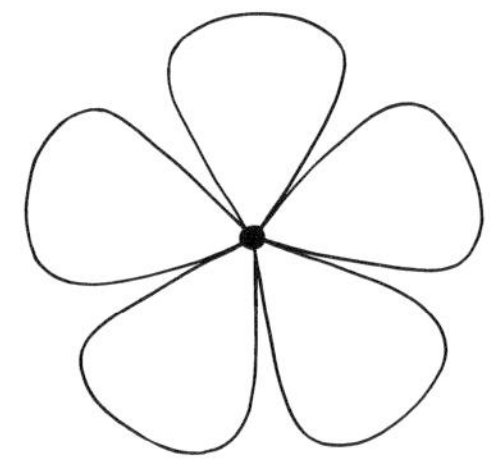

7. Colour $\frac{1}{4}$ yellow.
   Colour $\frac{1}{8}$ blue.
   Colour $\frac{1}{2}$ red.

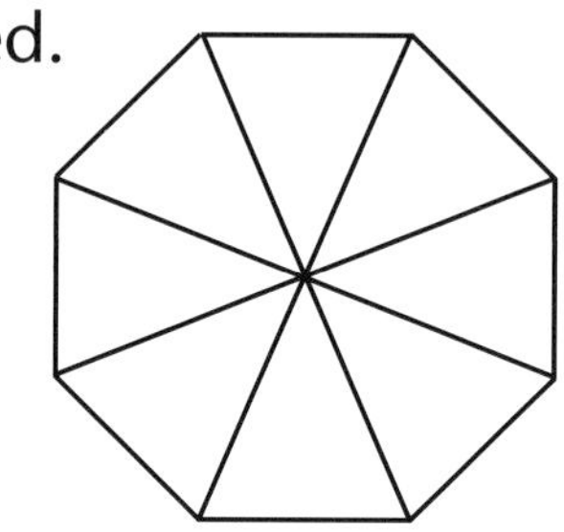

8. Divide this shape into eighths.

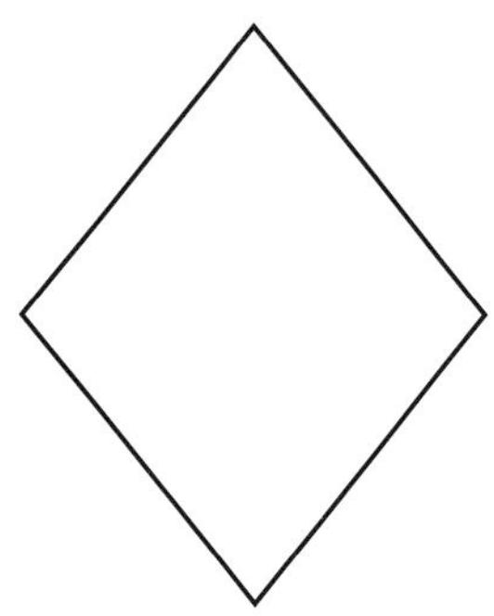

9. Show $\frac{1}{8}$ by colouring it green.

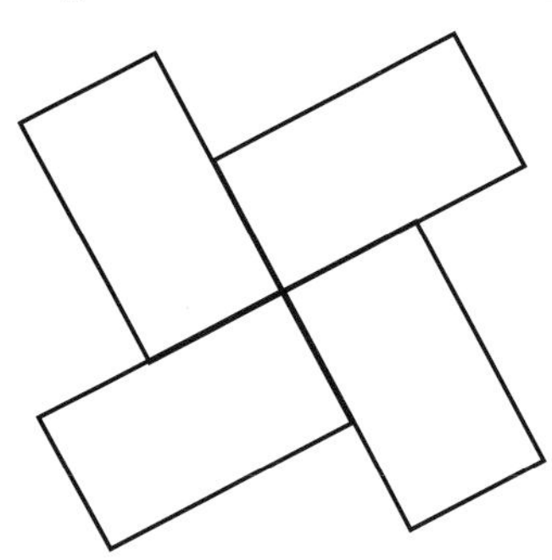

Ordering fractions and improper fractions

I am learning to order unit fractions.

A. Put these fractions in order from **smallest** to **biggest**.

1.

2.

3.

4.

5.

6.

7.

8.

9.

10.

B. What do you notice? ______________________________

____

I am learning to order improper fractions of a shape.

A. Room 5 pupils went to visit the chocolate factory. Each of them was allowed to eat some pieces of different chocolate bars. Complete the chart to show how many chocolate bars each pupil ate altogether.

1.	Jaeden	five halves	$\frac{5}{2}$	$2\frac{1}{2}$
2.	Mary		$\frac{17}{8}$	
3.	Tom	twenty-three tenths		
4.	Michael	eight thirds		
5.	Shay		$\frac{6}{4}$	
6.	Shannon			$3\frac{1}{2}$
7.	Christine	twelve fifths		
8.	Joseph	nine quarters		
9.	Isabella		$\frac{15}{10}$	
10.	Kate	nine eighths		
11.	Kerry		$\frac{9}{9}$	
12.	Neve			$3\frac{1}{5}$

B. Write the mixed fraction for each child beside their name. Cut up the cards and put them in order from **smallest** to **biggest** fraction.

Jaeden	**Mary**	**Tom**
Michael	**Shay**	**Shannon**
Christine	**Joseph**	**Isabella**
Kate	**Kerry**	**Neve**

I am learning to order fractions with the same denominators.

1. Who ate the most pizza? Cut the pizzas out and put them in order from **biggest** to **smallest**.

Theo	Tim	Tom
$\frac{3}{3}$ 	$\frac{1}{3}$ 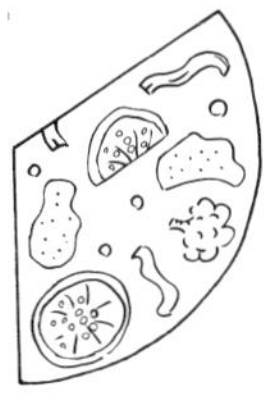	$\frac{2}{3}$ 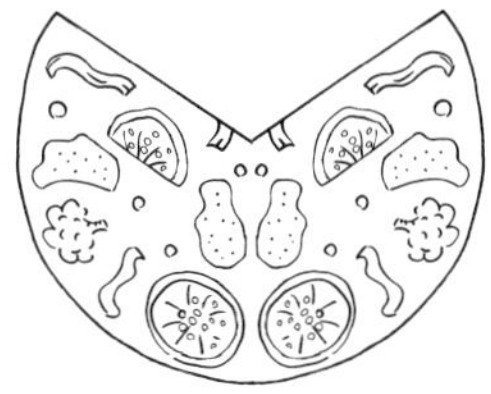

2. Who ate the most pizza? Cut the pizzas out and put in them order from **biggest** to **smallest**.

Wilber	Winston	Wilamina	Wendy
$\frac{3}{4}$ 	$\frac{1}{4}$ 	$\frac{2}{4}$ 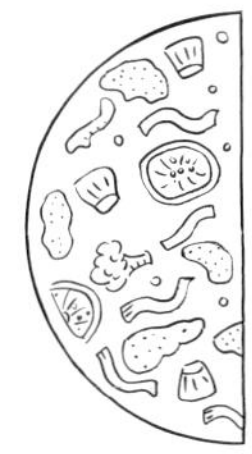	$\frac{4}{4}$ 

3. Who ate the most chocolate? Cut the chocolate bars out and put them in order from **biggest** to **smallest**.

Samuel	Sally	Suzi	Simon	Sonia
$\frac{4}{5}$ 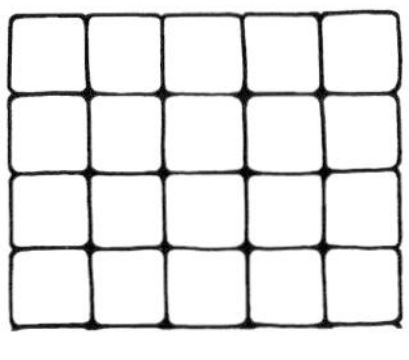	$\frac{2}{5}$ 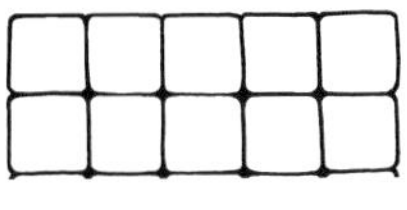	$\frac{3}{5}$ 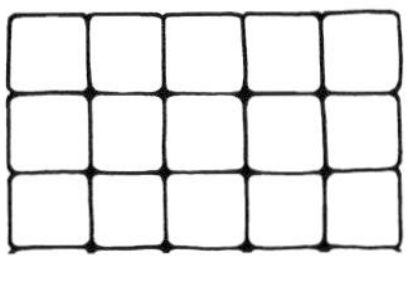	$\frac{1}{5}$ 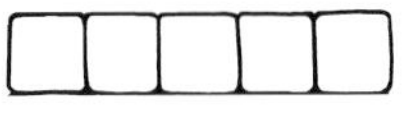	$\frac{5}{5}$ 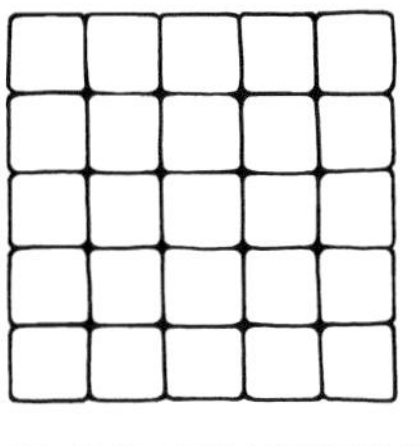

Finding a unit fraction of a continuous region

I am learning to find unit fractions of a continuous region.

A.

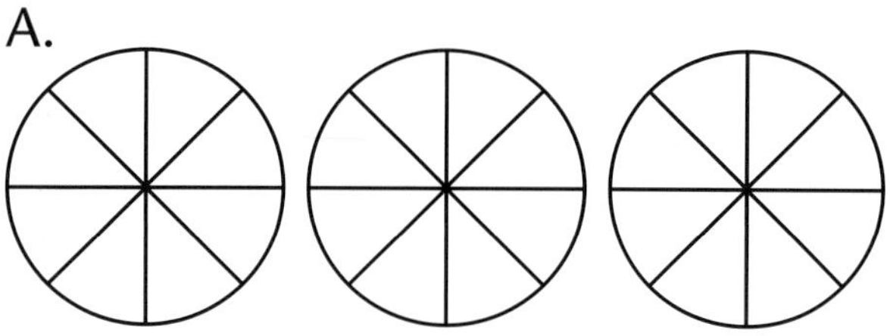

1. Colour $\frac{1}{8}$ 2. Colour $\frac{1}{4}$ 3. Colour $\frac{1}{2}$

C.

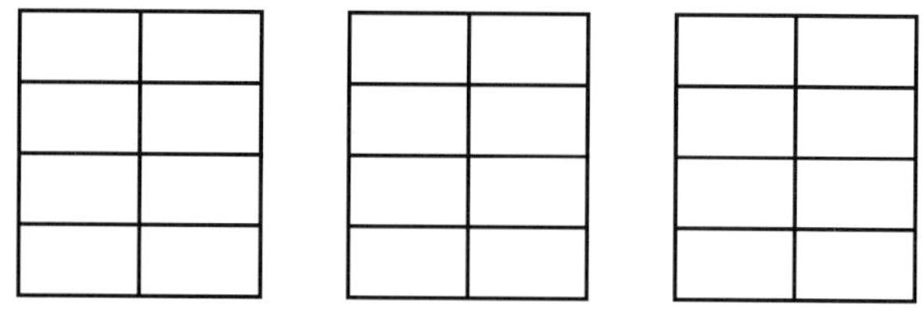

1. Colour $\frac{1}{8}$ 2. Colour $\frac{1}{4}$ 3. Colour $\frac{1}{2}$

B.

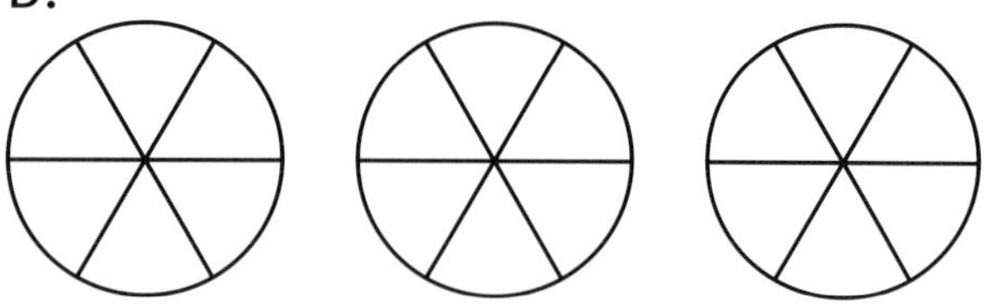

1. Colour $\frac{1}{6}$ 2. Colour $\frac{1}{2}$ 3. Colour $\frac{1}{3}$

D.

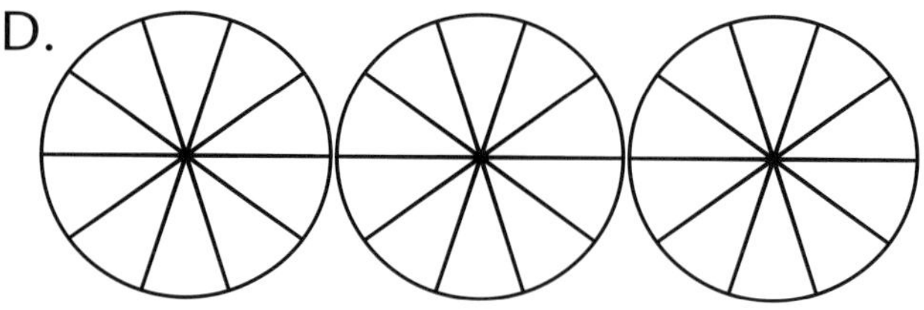

1. Colour $\frac{1}{2}$ 2. Colour $\frac{1}{5}$ 3. Colour $\frac{1}{10}$

E.

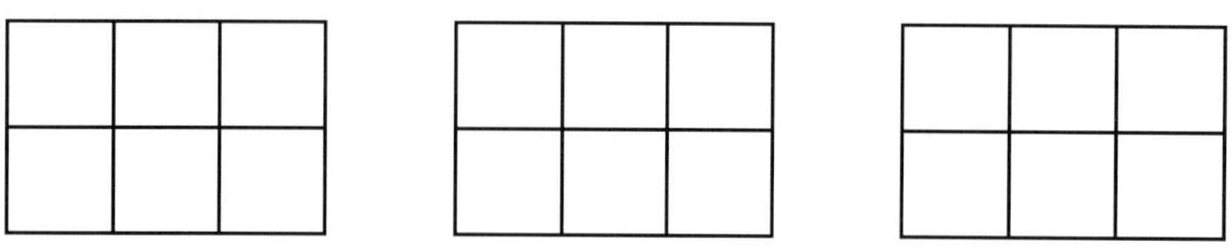

1. Colour $\frac{1}{6}$ 2. Colour $\frac{1}{2}$ 3. Colour $\frac{1}{3}$

F.

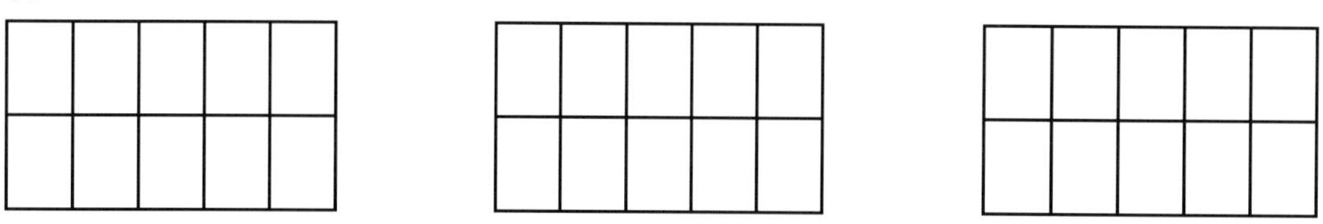

1. Colour $\frac{1}{2}$ 2. Colour $\frac{1}{5}$ 3. Colour $\frac{1}{10}$

G.

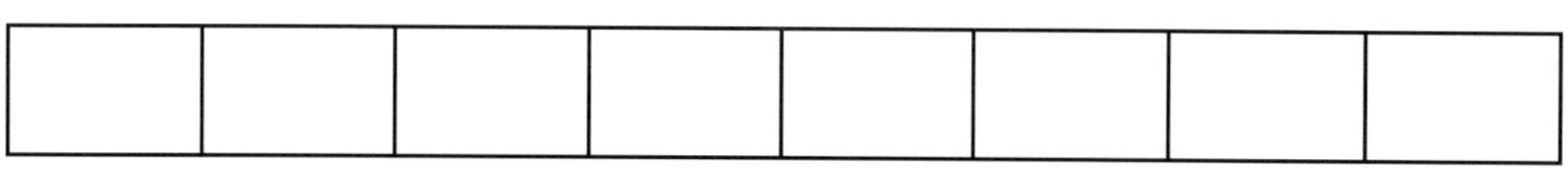

1. Colour $\frac{1}{8}$ in red, $\frac{1}{4}$ in blue and $\frac{1}{2}$ in green

H.

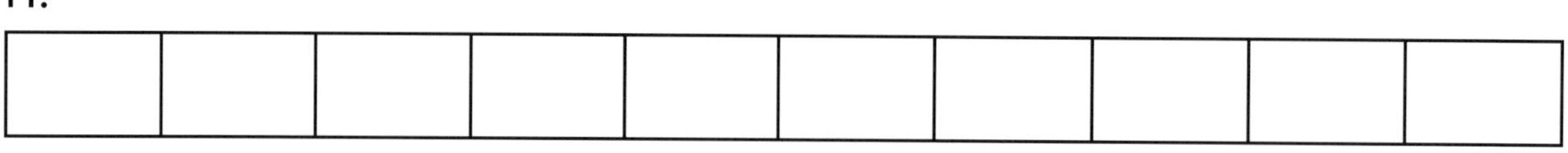

1. Colour $\frac{1}{5}$ in red, $\frac{1}{2}$ in blue and $\frac{1}{10}$ in green

Identifying decimal numbers up to 3 decimal places

I am learning to identify decimals up to 3 decimal places.

A. The school librarian has asked you to write a number code on each of these books. The first one is done for you.

1. five point nine five four
2. eight point three five four
3. two point two six six
4. nine point one nine nine
5. four point eight six five
6. three point one two three
7. one point four two one
8. seven point three eight nine
9. zero point zero three two

B. Write the number name next to the number. Use the list to help you.

1.	14.382	
2.	6.412	
3.	8.593	
4.	36.159	
5.	4.628	
6.	3.258	
7.	8.947	
8.	5.109	
9.	7.942	
10.	6.854	
11.	9.021	
12.	72.036	
13.	81.105	
14.	62.304	

thirty-six point one five nine
three point two five eight
four point six two eight
eighty-one point one zero five
nine point zero two one
seven point nine four two
seventy-two point zero three six
six point eight five four
fourteen point three eight two
eight point nine four seven
sixty-two point three zero four
six point four one two
five point one zero nine
eight point five nine three

I am learning to identify decimals up to 3 decimal places.

A. Match each number to the correct number name.

1.	6.329	six point thirty-two nine
		six point three hundred and twenty-nine
		six point three two nine
2.	8.068	eight point sixty-eight
		eight point zero six eight
		eight point zero sixty-eight
3.	2.459	two point four five nine
		two point four hundred and fifty-nine
		two point forty fifty-nine
4.	7.208	seven point two eight
		seven point two zero eight
		seven point two hundred and eight
5.	9.518	nine point five hundred and eighteen
		nine point fifty-one eight
		nine point five one eight

B. Write the number name for these numbers.

1.	83.698	
2.	5.267	
3.	14.251	
4.	6.025	
5.	37.003	
6.	90.017	

Rounding decimals

I am learning to round decimals with up to two decimal places to the nearest whole number.

Round each of these numbers to the nearest whole number.

1. 67.45	2. 34.67	3. 24.09	4. 62.78	5. 26.42	6. 73.39
7. 28.67	8. 17.98	9. 56.34	10. 35.26	11. 28.59	12. 54.04
13. 62.63	14. 89.72	15. 65.32	16. 24.63	17. 47.66	18. 133.04
19. 59.72	20. 45.78	21. 71.67	22. 308.47	23. 836.18	24. 42.09
25. 96.76	26. 664.54	27. 61.31	28. 8.27	29. 67.58	30. 12.83

I am learning to round decimals with up to two decimal places to the nearest whole number.

Round each of these numbers to the nearest whole number.

1. 265.84	2. 21.94	3. 49.63	4. 72.85	5. 93.42	6. 751.92
7. 27.93	8. 382.18	9. 78.69	10. 59.85	11. 98.49	12. 8.96
13. 540.74	14. 99.72	15. 13.09	16. 87.04	17. 380.06	18. 409.77
19. 12.95	20. 27.38	21. 509.56	22. 46.31	23. 19.22	24. 78.45
25. 39.79	26. 46.51	27. 47.87	28. 368.68	29. 54.09	30. 155.04

Learning more about ordering fractions

I am learning to order fractions for halves, quarters, thirds, fifths and tenths.

A. Match the pizza pieces to the children. Match them so that the biggest child gets the biggest piece and the smallest child gets the smallest piece.

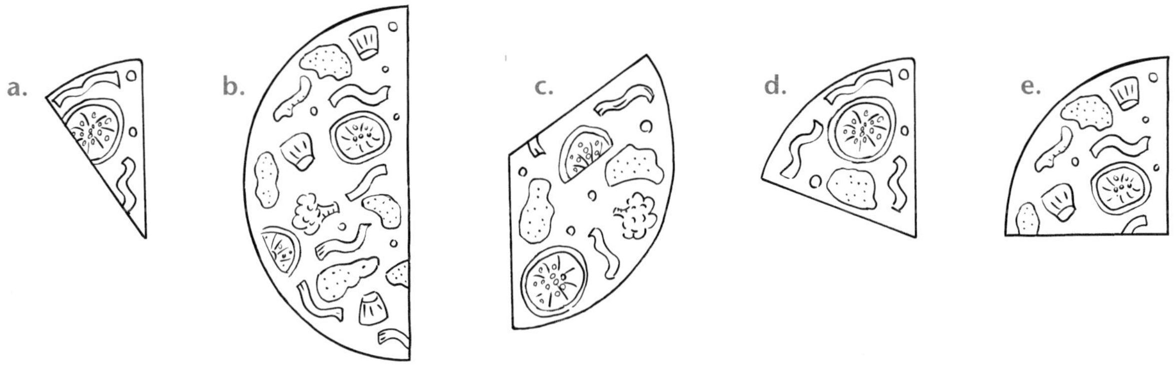

B. Write the unit fractions in order from **biggest** to **smallest**. What do you notice?

$\frac{1}{5}$ $\frac{1}{4}$ $\frac{1}{2}$ $\frac{1}{10}$ $\frac{1}{3}$

________ ________ ________ ________ ________

____

C. James and Julia went to the movies. They shared a chocolate bar. Julia ate $\frac{1}{3}$, James ate $\frac{1}{5}$.

1. Who ate the most? __________

Ravi, John and Latoya shared a bag of lollies. Ravi ate $\frac{1}{10}$, John ate $\frac{1}{5}$ and Latoya ate $\frac{1}{2}$.

2. Who ate the least? __________

3. Who ate the most? __________

Simon and Ethan went to the movies. They shared a chocolate bar. Simon ate $\frac{1}{4}$, Ethan ate $\frac{1}{8}$.

4. Who ate the most? __________

Wil, Riley and Neave shared a bag of lollies. Wil ate $\frac{1}{3}$, Riley ate $\frac{1}{6}$ and Neave ate $\frac{1}{9}$.

5. Who ate the least? __________

6. Who ate the most? __________

Finding fractions of continuous shapes

I am learning use symmetry to find fractions of continuous shapes.

1. Find and mark $\frac{1}{2}$ of the shape. Colour $\frac{1}{4}$ red.

2. Find and mark $\frac{1}{3}$ of the shape. Colour $\frac{1}{6}$ blue.

3. Find and mark $\frac{1}{4}$ of the shape. Colour $\frac{1}{8}$ green.

4. Find and mark $\frac{1}{3}$ of the rectangle. Colour $\frac{1}{6}$ green.

5. Find and mark $\frac{1}{2}$ of the rectangle. Colour $\frac{1}{4}$ blue.

6. Find and mark $\frac{1}{4}$ of the rectangle. Colour $\frac{1}{8}$ red.

7. Find and mark $\frac{1}{3}$ of the rectangle. Find and mark $\frac{1}{6}$ and colour $\frac{1}{12}$ yellow.

8. Find and mark $\frac{1}{2}$ of the circle. Find and mark $\frac{1}{4}$ and colour $\frac{1}{8}$ green.

9. Find and mark $\frac{1}{3}$ of the circle. Find and mark $\frac{1}{6}$ and colour $\frac{1}{12}$ green.

10. Find and mark $\frac{1}{4}$ of the circle and colour $\frac{1}{8}$ green.

Identifying symbols for tenths and hundredths

I am learning to identify symbols for tenths and hundredths including those greater than one.

Cut out all the parts and match the correct pieces together to make fraction families. The first one is done for you.

1.	$\frac{83}{100}$	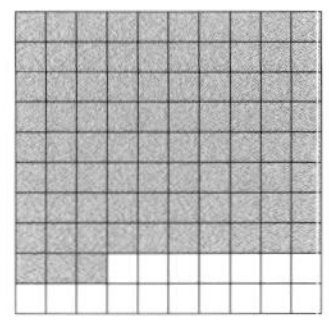	83 hundredths
2.	$\frac{21}{100}$	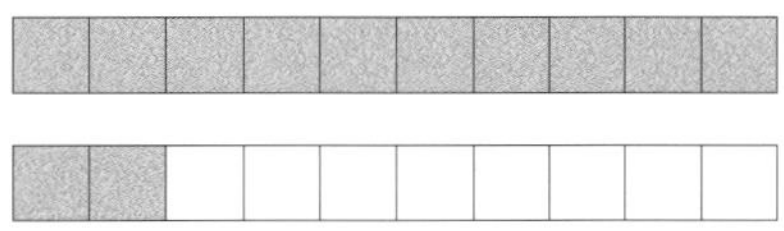	17 tenths
3.	$\frac{6}{10}$		124 hundredths
4.	$\frac{17}{10}$	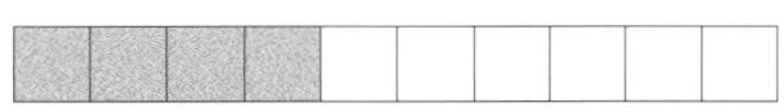	21 hundredths
5.	$\frac{145}{100}$	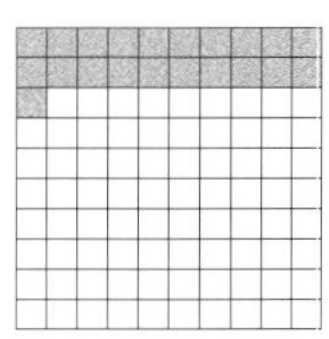	145 hundredths
6.	$\frac{4}{10}$	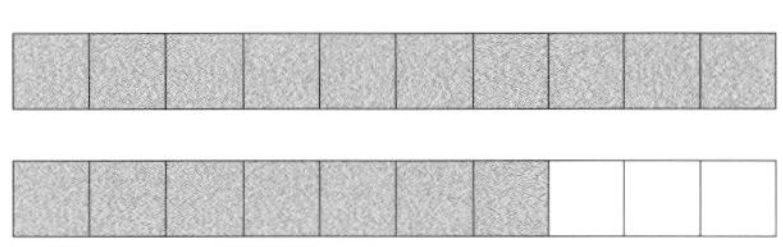	12 tenths
7.	$\frac{124}{100}$	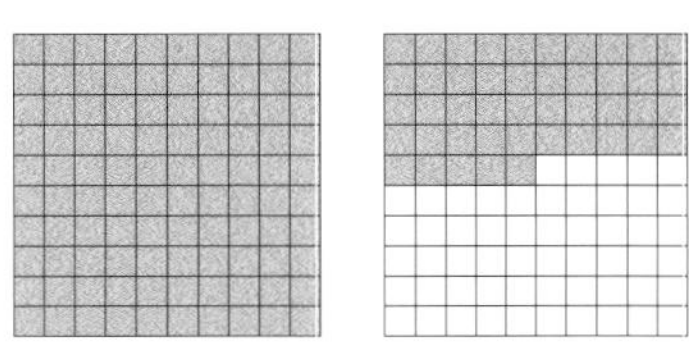	6 tenths
8.	$\frac{12}{10}$	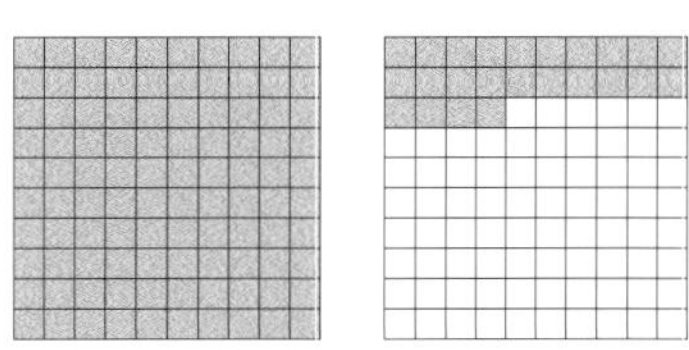	4 tenths

Counting on and back in fractions and decimals

I am learning to count forwards and backwards in $\frac{1}{2}$, $\frac{1}{3}$, $\frac{1}{4}$, $\frac{1}{5}$ and $\frac{1}{10}$.

1. Fill in the missing fractions. Count back in **tenths**.

2. Fill in the missing fractions. Count on or back in **halves**.

3. Fill in the missing fractions. Count on or back in **quarters**.

4. Fill in the missing fractions. Count back in **fifths**.

5. Fill in the missing fractions. Count on or back in **thirds**.

I am learning to count forwards and backwards in $\frac{1}{2}$, $\frac{1}{3}$, $\frac{1}{4}$, $\frac{1}{5}$ and $\frac{1}{10}$.

1. Fill in the missing fractions. Count on or back in **tenths**.

2. Fill in the missing fractions. Count on or back in **halves**.

3. Fill in the missing fractions. Count back in **quarters**.

4. Fill in the missing fractions. Count back in **thirds**.

5. Fill in the missing fractions. Count on or back in **fifths**.

I am learning to count forwards and backwards in $\frac{1}{2}$, $\frac{1}{3}$, $\frac{1}{4}$, $\frac{1}{5}$ and $\frac{1}{10}$.

1. Fill in the missing fractions. Count on or back in **fifths**.

2. Fill in the missing fractions. Count on or back in **quarters**.

3. Fill in the missing fractions. Count on or back in **thirds**.

4. Fill in the missing fractions. Count on or back in **tenths**.

5. Fill in the missing fractions. Count on or back in **halves**.

I am learning to count forwards and backwards in tenths.

A. Fill in the blank squares in each grid.

1.

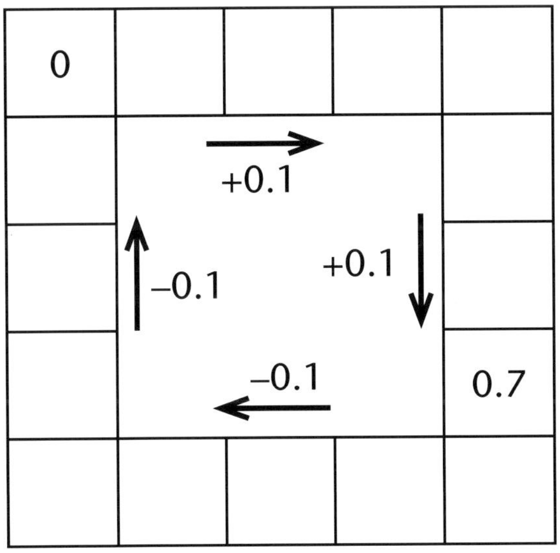

2.

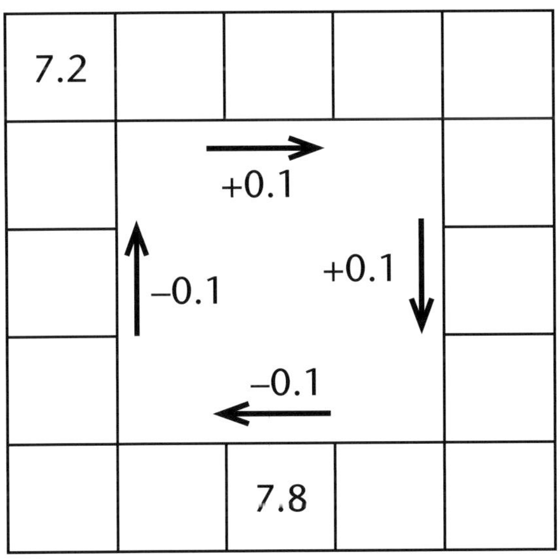

3.

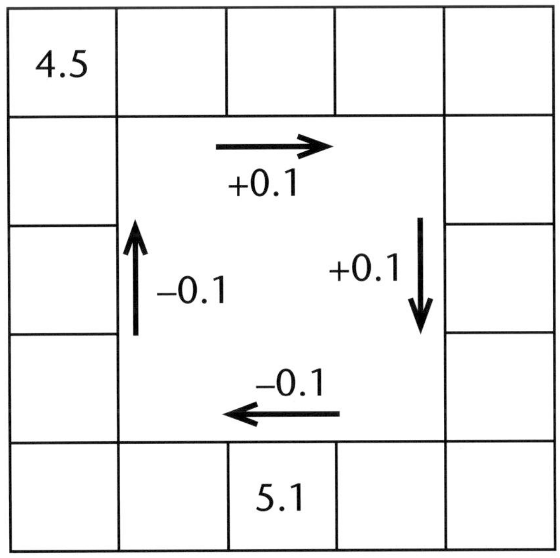

4.

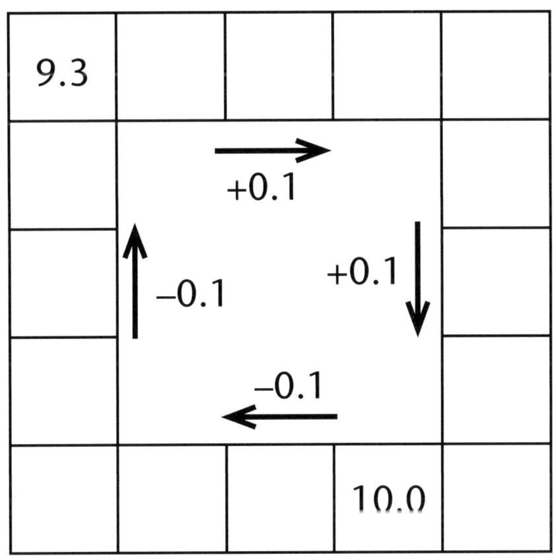

B. Write in two numbers on each grid sheet below. Then see if a friend can complete your grid sheets.

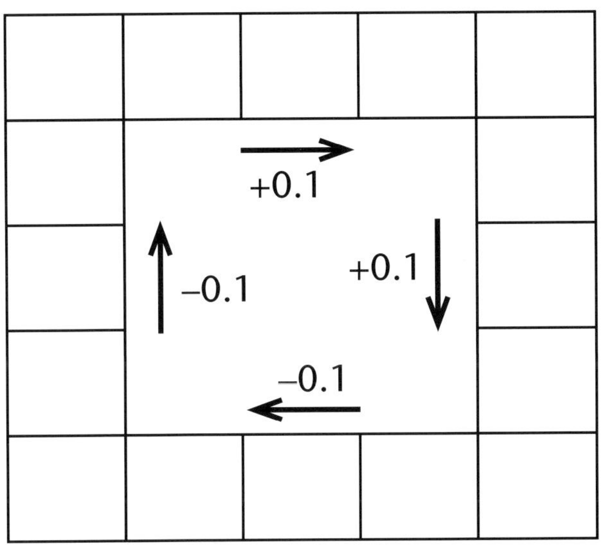

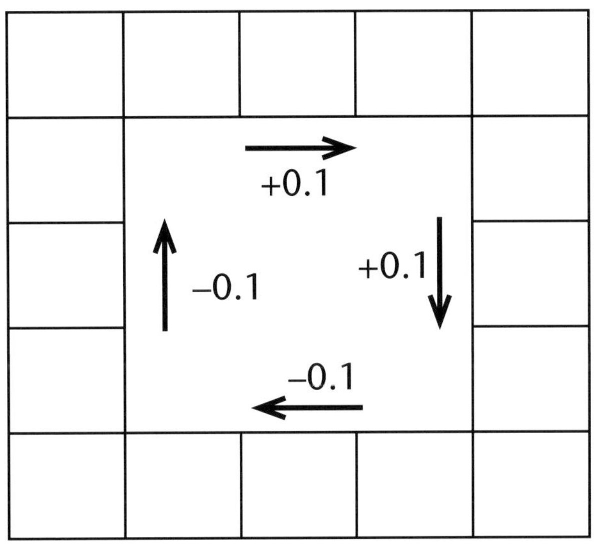

I am learning to count forwards and backwards in hundredths.

A. Fill in the blank squares in each grid.

1.

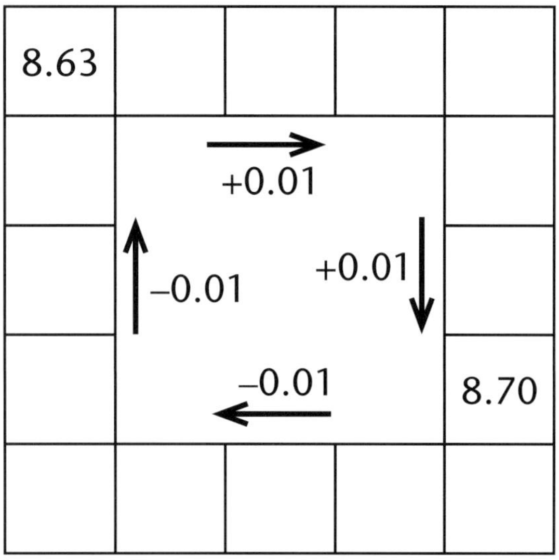

2.

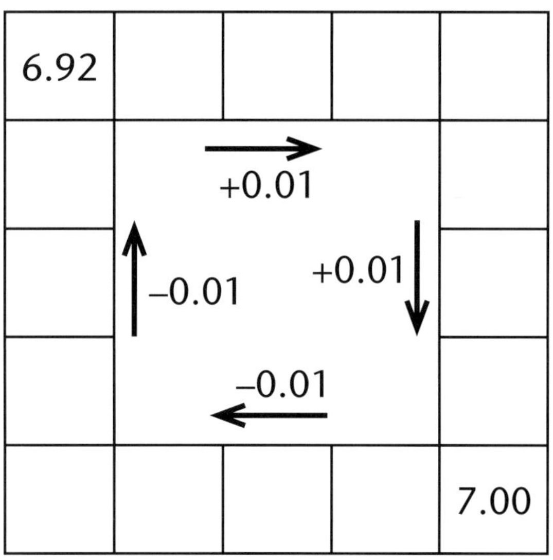

3.

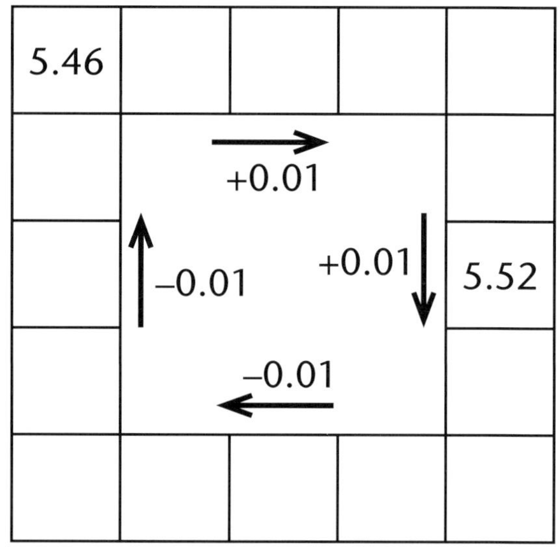

4.

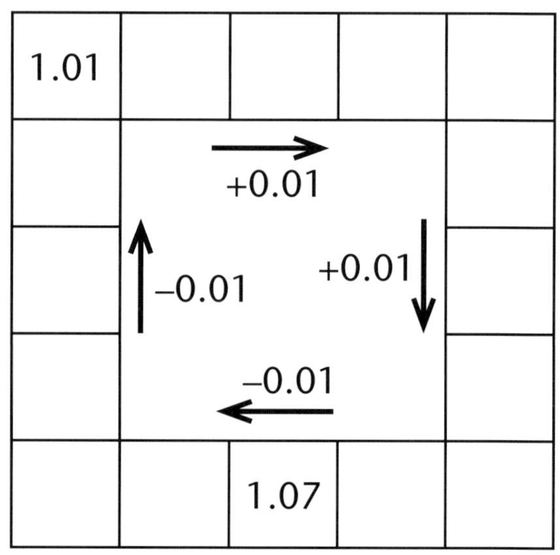

B. Write in two numbers on each grid sheet below. Then see if a friend can complete your grid sheets.

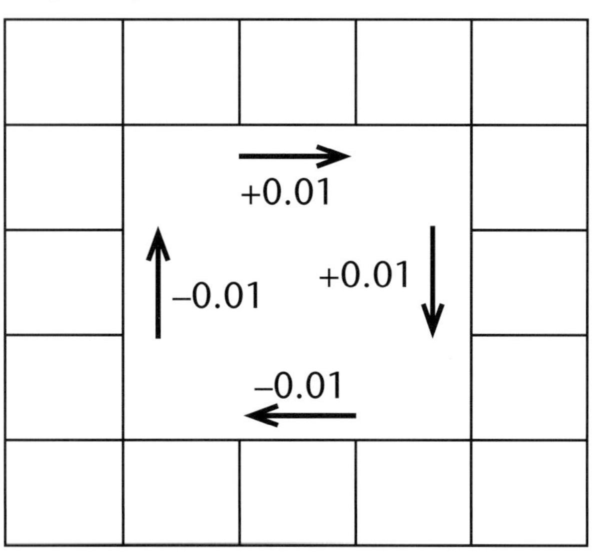

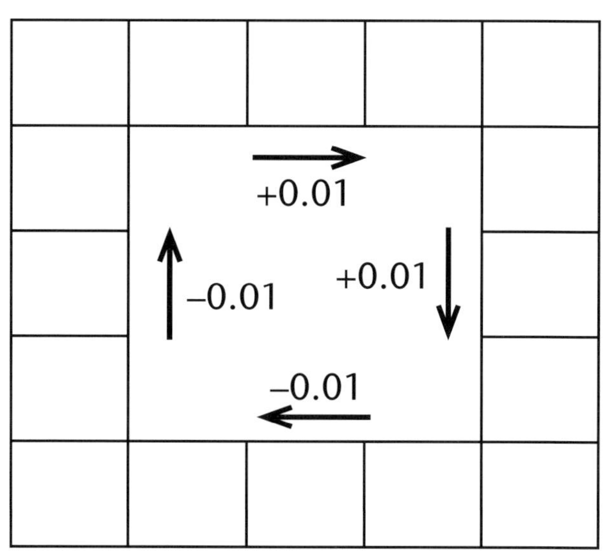

I am learning to count forwards and backwards in tenths and hundredths.

Fill in the blank squares.

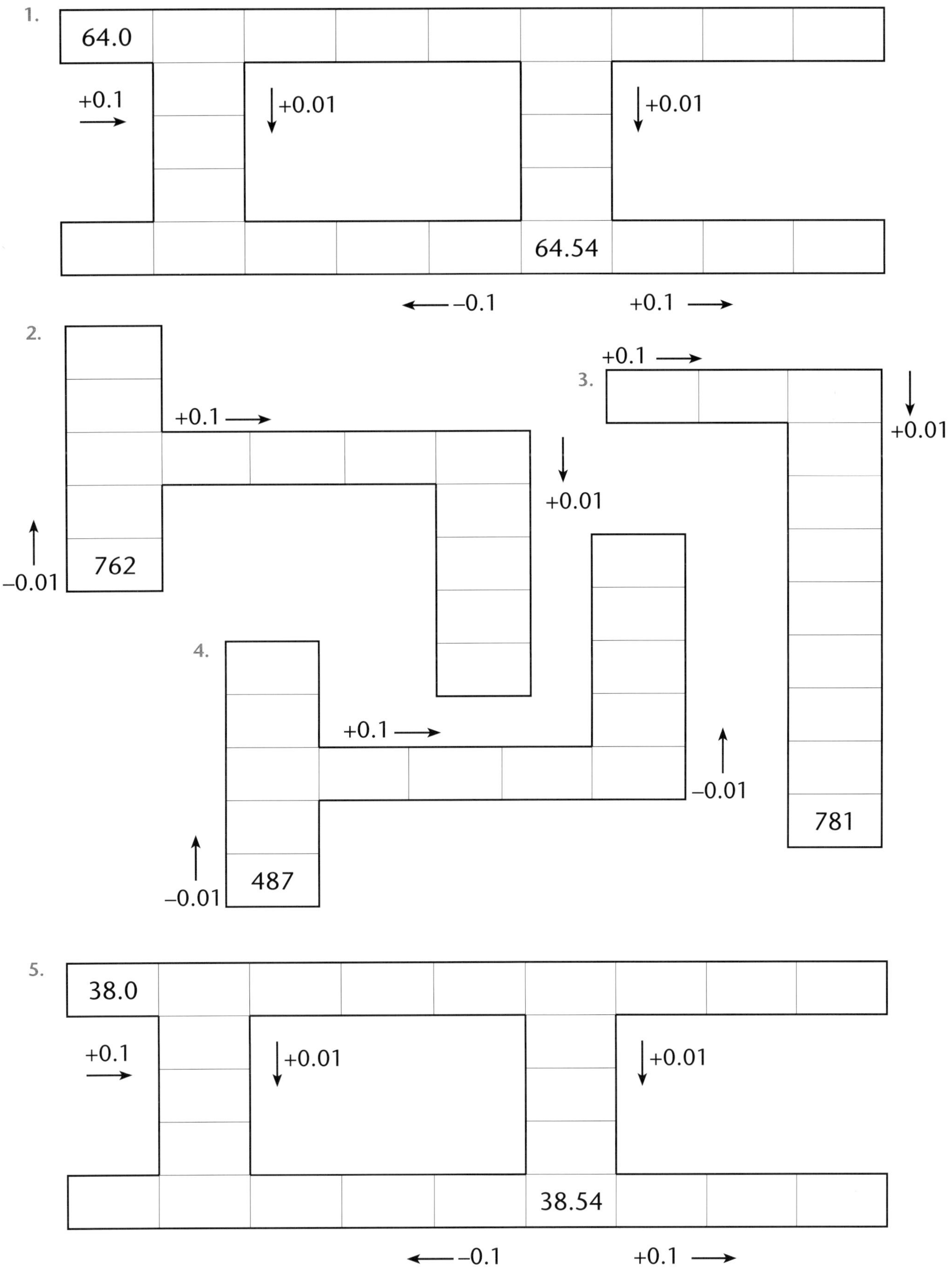

I am learning to count forwards in tenths.

Write the number that each shape is covering and the two numbers that come after it.

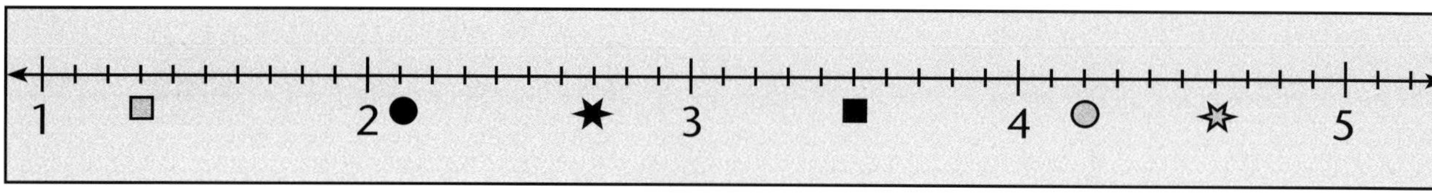

1. ■ = ____ , ____ , ____
2. ★ = ____ , ____ , ____
3. ○ = ____ , ____ , ____
4. ● = ____ , ____ , ____
5. ■ = ____ , ____ , ____
6. ✡ = ____ , ____ , ____

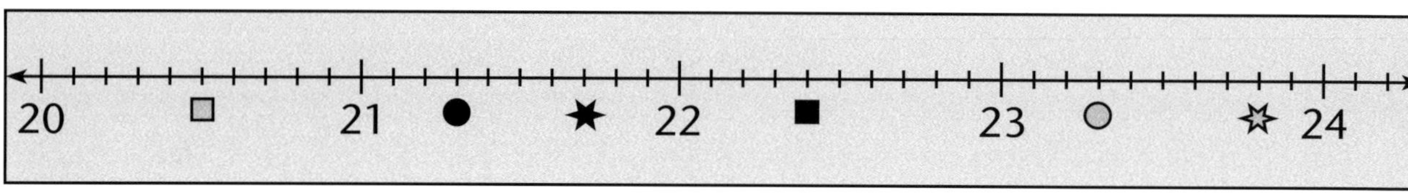

7. ■ = ____ , ____ , ____
8. ★ = ____ , ____ , ____
9. ○ = ____ , ____ , ____
10. ● = ____ , ____ , ____
11. ■ = ____ , ____ , ____
12. ✡ = ____ , ____ , ____

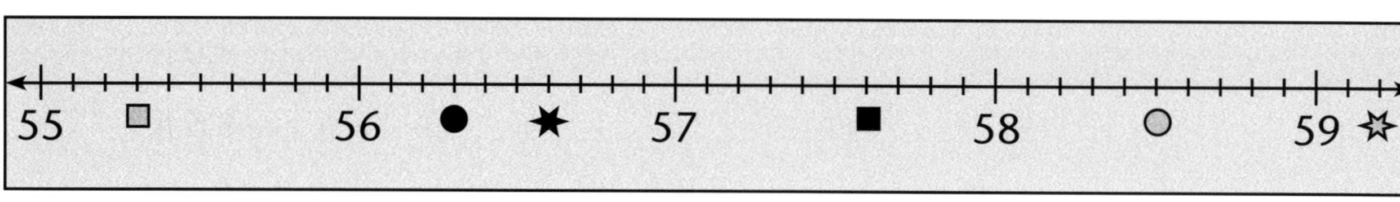

13. ■ = ____ , ____ , ____
14. ★ = ____ , ____ , ____
15. ○ = ____ , ____ , ____
16. ● = ____ , ____ , ____
17. ■ = ____ , ____ , ____
18. ✡ = ____ , ____ , ____

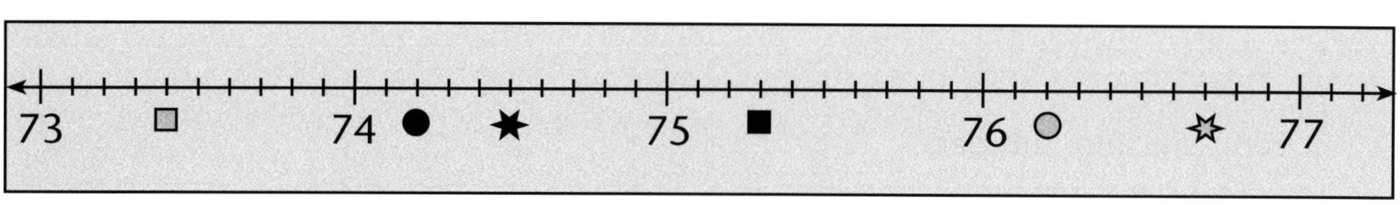

19. ■ = ____ , ____ , ____
20. ★ = ____ , ____ , ____
21. ○ = ____ , ____ , ____
22. ● = ____ , ____ , ____
23. ■ = ____ , ____ , ____
24. ✡ = ____ , ____ , ____

I am learning to count on in tenths.

A. In these charts, each column is one tenth more than the column before it. Fill in the missing numbers.

	Before	Between	After
1.		8.3	
2.		3.6	
3.		5.9	
4.		7.2	
5.		7.5	
6.		4.0	
7.		1.3	
8.		2.6	
9.		4.8	
10.		9.5	

	Before	Between	After
11.		6.3	
12.	8.4		
13.			9.7
14.		5.2	
15.	7.3		
16.		8.0	
17.			6.8
18.		2.9	
19.	4.1		
20.		3.7	

B. Using the charts above, complete the following sentences.

1. The number before 4.8 is ________
2. The number after 7.5 is ________
3. The number before 3.6 is ________
4. The number after 4.1 is ________
5. The number after 8.3 is ________
6. The number between 1.2 and 1.4 is ________
7. The number between 7.9 and 8.1 is ________
8. The number between 2.5 and 2.7 is ________
9. The number before 3.0 is ________
10. The number before 8.5 is ________
11. The number after 2.9 is ________
12. The number before 9.6 is ________

C. Fill in the missing numbers.

1.

	6.4				6.8		

2.

				9.4			9.7

I am learning to count on and back in tenths.

A. In these charts, each column is one tenth more than the column before it.
Fill in the missing numbers.

	Before	Between	After
1.		12.06	
2.		57.15	
3.		40.06	
4.		83.21	
5.		96.49	
6.		21.52	
7.		13.85	
8.		49.36	
9.		86.42	
10.		30.27	

	Before	Between	After
11.		27.03	
12.	68.42		
13.		94.63	
14.			58.31
15.		52.12	
16.	94.69		
17.		12.38	
18.			60.04
19.	51.75		
20.		21.09	

B. Using the charts above, complete the following sentences.

1. The number before 21.19 is ______
2. The number after 40.06 is ______
3. The number before 58.31 is ______
4. The number before 68.62 is ______
5. The number after 52.02 is ______
6. The number between 52.02 and 52.22 is ______
7. The number between 68.42 and 68.62 is ______
8. The number between 39.96 and 40.16 is ______
9. The number before 96.59 is ______
10. The number before 13.95 is ______
11. The number before 21.19 is ______
12. The number before 57.25 is ______
13. The number before 27.13 is ______

C. Fill in the missing numbers.

1.

	9.60				10.00		

2.

				6.01			6.31

Working on more strategies to find a fraction of a set

I am learning to find a fraction of a set using multiplication and division.

A. Complete the number machines.

$\frac{1}{3}$ of

1. 6 → ____
2. 24 → ____
3. 9 → ____
4. 18 → ____
5. 27 → ____
6. 12 → ____

$\frac{1}{4}$ of

13. 40 → ____
14. 12 → ____
15. 24 → ____
16. 16 → ____
17. 36 → ____
18. 20 → ____

$\frac{1}{5}$ of

7. 10 → ____
8. 45 → ____
9. 25 → ____
10. 50 → ____
11. 30 → ____
12. 15 → ____

$\frac{1}{8}$ of

19. 72 → ____
20. 56 → ____
21. 48 → ____
22. 64 → ____
23. 40 → ____
24. 16 → ____

B. Fill in the missing number to complete each problem.

1. $\frac{1}{8}$ of ____ is 6.
2. $\frac{1}{5}$ of ____ is 4.
3. $\frac{1}{3}$ of ____ is 9.
4. $\frac{1}{6}$ of ____ is 5.
5. $\frac{1}{4}$ of ____ is 8.
6. $\frac{1}{5}$ of ____ is 9.
7. $\frac{1}{3}$ of ____ is 10.
8. $\frac{1}{6}$ of ____ is 6.

C. Fill in the missing denominators.

1. $\frac{1}{\square} \times 80 = 8$
2. $\frac{1}{\square} \times 42 = 6$
3. $\frac{1}{\square} \times 63 = 7$
4. $\frac{1}{\square} \times 36 = 9$

I am learning to find a fraction of a set using multiplication and division.

A. Work out if each problem is true or false and justify your answer.

1. $\frac{2}{3} \times 45 = 18$	4. $\frac{3}{4} \times 24 = 12$	7. $\frac{2}{3} \times 36 = 27$
TRUE / FALSE	TRUE / FALSE	TRUE / FALSE
WHY?	WHY?	WHY?
2. $\frac{5}{8} \times 56 = 35$	5. $\frac{4}{5} \times 23 = 15$	8. $\frac{3}{8} \times 32 = 12$
TRUE / FALSE	TRUE / FALSE	TRUE / FALSE
WHY?	WHY?	WHY?
3. $\frac{3}{4} \times 36 = 27$	6. $\frac{2}{3} \times 15 = 10$	9. $\frac{7}{8} \times 40 = 35$
TRUE / FALSE	TRUE / FALSE	TRUE / FALSE
WHY?	WHY?	WHY?

B. Fill in the missing number to complete each problem.

1. $\frac{4}{5} \times$ _____ $= 8$
3. $\frac{3}{4} \times$ _____ $= 24$
5. $\frac{5}{8} \times$ _____ $= 35$
7. $\frac{2}{3} \times$ _____ $= 16$
2. $\frac{2}{3} \times 9 =$ _____
4. $\frac{7}{8} \times 56 =$ _____
6. $\frac{3}{5} \times 45 =$ _____
8. $\frac{3}{4} \times 36 =$ _____

I am learning to find a fraction of a set using multiplication and division.

A. Mum made a huge fruit salad for the school fair, using some of the fruit from her fruit bowl. What fraction of each kind of fruit did she use? Write your answer as a simple fraction.

	Kind of fruit	Total in bowl	Mum used	Fraction
1.	Bananas	24	6	
2.	Apples	12	8	
3.	Grapes	60	36	
4.	Pears	33	11	
5.	Kiwifruit	28	21	
6.	Cherries	72	48	

7. She also had a 5 L bottle of apple juice and poured 500 ml into the fruit salad.

What fraction of juice did she use? ______

B. We raised a total of £4 800.00 at the fair through various activities. What fraction of this total did each activity raise? Write your answer as a simple fraction.

	Fair activity	Amount raised	Fraction of total
1.	Donations	£2 400	
2.	Lucky dip	£600	
3.	Bouncy castle	£400	
4.	Waterslide	£200	
5.	Food	£1 200	

C. After the fair we cleaned up all the rubbish. We filled 24 rubbish bags in total but we filled each bag with just one kind of rubbish. What fraction of the total of rubbish bags held each kind of rubbish? Write your answer as a simple fraction.

	Contents of bags	Amount of bags	Fraction of total
1.	Glass bottles	8	
2.	Paper	6	
3.	Plastic	4	

Solving division problems with fraction answers

I am learning to solve division problems that have fraction answers using halving.

A. Find out how much pizza each person will eat.

1. Each person will have _____ pizzas.

2. Each person will have _____ pizzas.

3. Each person will have _____ pizzas.

B. Solve these problems.
Write your answer as a simple fraction. The first one is done for you.

1. $5 \div 2 = \frac{5}{2} = 2\frac{1}{2}$
2. $12 \div 10 =$
3. $5 \div 4 =$
4. $6 \div 8 =$
5. $9 \div 12 =$
6. $8 \div 6 =$
7. $3 \div 4 =$
8. $9 \div 4 =$
9. $4 \div 3 =$
10. $7 \div 4 =$
11. $8 \div 5 =$
12. $10 \div 6 =$
13. $2 \div 3 =$

Measuring unit fractions within whole numbers

I am learning to measure how many times a unit fraction goes into a whole number.

Help the children cut up their straps of raspberry liquorice into quarters.

1.

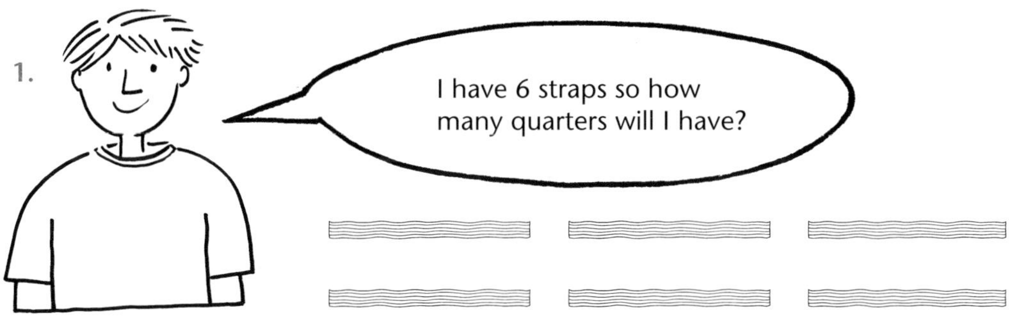

2.

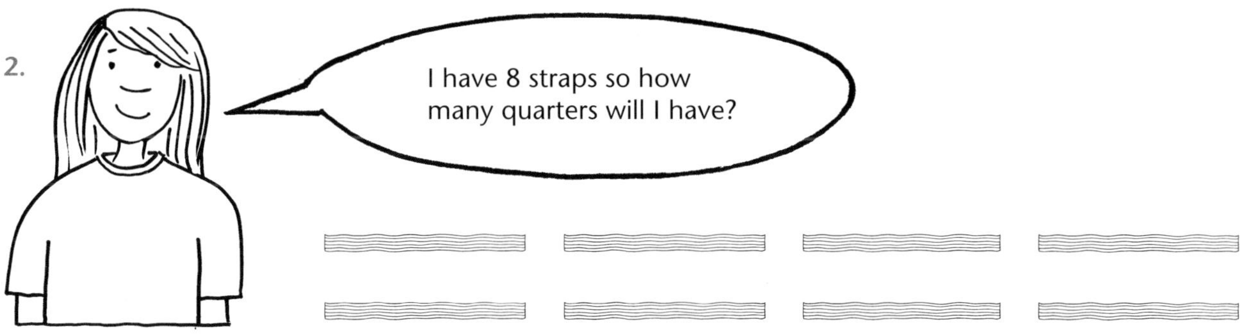

3.

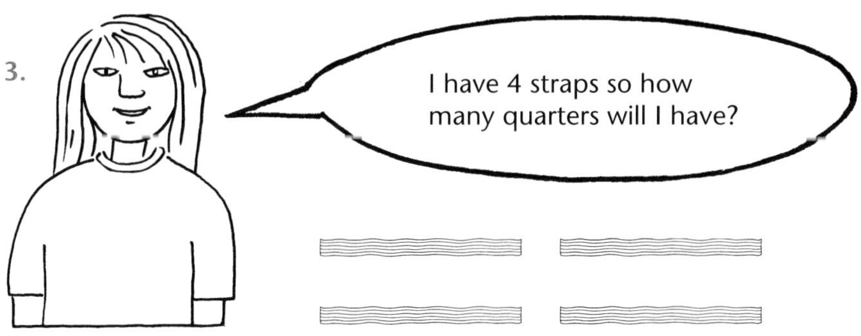

4.

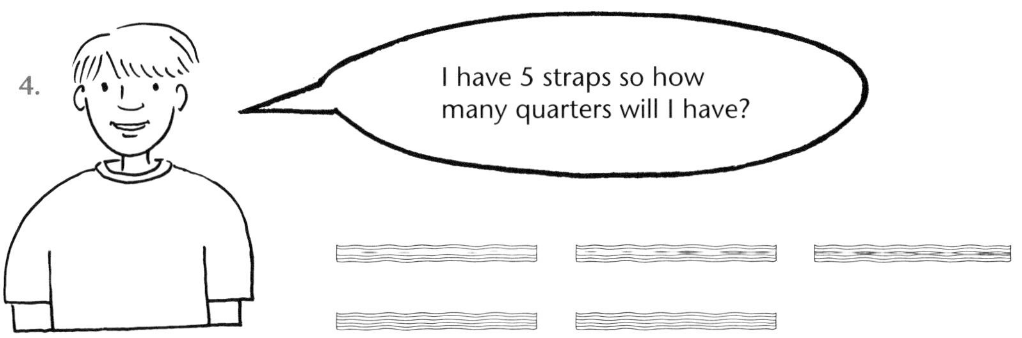

I am learning to measure how many times a unit fraction goes into a whole number.

Help the children share out the orange juice. They will put a quarter of a litre in each glass. Now answer these questions.

1. 5 bottles equals _____ quarters.

2. 4 bottles equals _____ quarters.

3. 7 bottles equals _____ quarters.

4. 3 bottles equals _____ quarters.

5. 6 glasses equals _____ bottles.

6. 10 glasses equals _____ bottles.

7. 27 glasses equals _____ bottles.

8. 19 glasses equals _____ bottles.

I am learning to measure how many times a unit fraction goes into a whole number.

Each room at St Teresa's is making cakes and sweets for the school fair.

A. Each cake uses one quarter of a kilogram of flour. How many cakes can each class make?

Room	Flour	Cakes
1	5 kg	
2	4 kg	
3	9 kg	
4	3 kg	
5	7 kg	
6	8 kg	
7	6 kg	
8	2 kg	
9	11 kg	
10	10 kg	

B. Each batch of sweets uses half a bag of sugar. How many bags of sugar did each class use?

Room	Sugar	Sweets
1		9
2		12
3		16
4		25
5		36
6		18
7		15
8		27
9		13
10		8

C. Ben's Orchard has donated large bags of apples. Each bag of Ben's apples fills five of the school's fruit boxes. Complete the table.

Room	Fruit boxes	Bags of apples
1	10	
2	20	
3	15	
4	18	

Working with improper fractions

I am learning to position improper fractions on a numberline.

Put these fractions in the correct place on the numberline.

1.
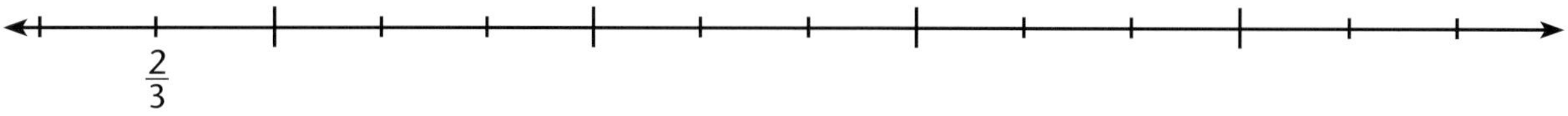

$\frac{5}{3}, \frac{8}{3}, \frac{1}{3}, \frac{10}{3}, \frac{7}{3}, \frac{3}{3}, \frac{12}{3}, \frac{9}{3}$

2.
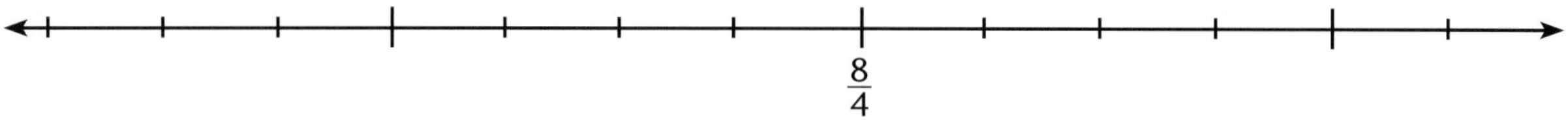

$\frac{2}{4}, \frac{11}{4}, \frac{4}{4}, \frac{12}{4}, \frac{5}{4}, \frac{9}{4}, \frac{13}{4}, \frac{7}{4}$

3.
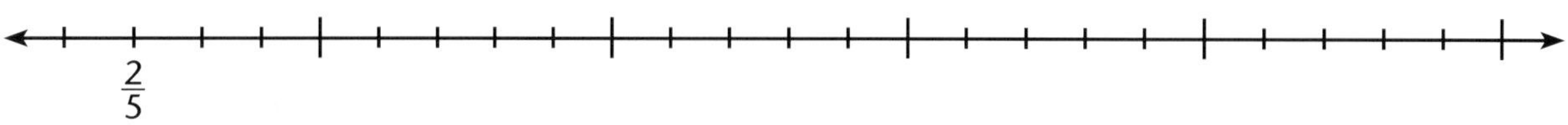

$\frac{10}{5}, \frac{6}{5}, \frac{14}{5}, \frac{20}{5}, \frac{17}{5}, \frac{4}{5}, \frac{8}{5}, \frac{16}{5}$

4.
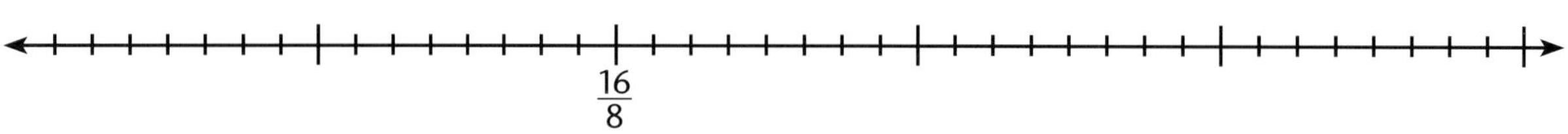

$\frac{7}{8}, \frac{24}{8}, \frac{14}{8}, \frac{20}{8}, \frac{11}{8}, \frac{3}{8}, \frac{17}{8}, \frac{27}{8}$

5.
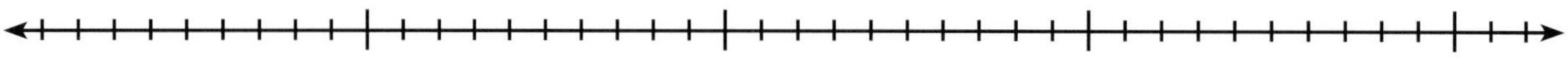

$\frac{8}{10}, \frac{20}{10}, \frac{35}{10}, \frac{2}{10}, \frac{30}{10}, \frac{25}{10}, \frac{12}{10}, \frac{39}{10}$

I am learning to rename improper fractions

Complete the tables.

	Improper fraction	Mixed fraction	Simple fraction
1.	$\frac{6}{4}$	$1\frac{2}{4}$	$1\frac{1}{2}$
2.	$\frac{7}{5}$		
3.		$2\frac{1}{3}$	
4.		$3\frac{2}{6}$	
5.	$\frac{18}{8}$		
6.		$1\frac{3}{4}$	
7.	$\frac{13}{5}$		
8.	$\frac{8}{3}$		
9.		$2\frac{2}{5}$	
10.	$\frac{21}{6}$		
11.	$\frac{9}{4}$		
12.		$\frac{6}{8}$	
13.	$\frac{13}{3}$		

	Improper fraction	Mixed fraction	Simple fraction
14.		$1\frac{2}{3}$	
15.	$\frac{8}{4}$		
16.		$3\frac{4}{6}$	
17.	$\frac{8}{5}$		
18.	$\frac{10}{3}$		
19.		$1\frac{4}{5}$	
20.	$\frac{34}{8}$		
21.	$\frac{4}{3}$		
22.		$3\frac{1}{5}$	
23.	$\frac{36}{10}$		
24.		$3\frac{2}{4}$	
25.	$\frac{14}{5}$		
26.		$3\frac{2}{3}$	

I am learning to rename improper fractions as mixed numbers with multiplication.

Change each improper fraction to a mixed fraction and place it on the numberline. The first one is started for you.

1. $\frac{3}{3} =$ 1
2. $\frac{8}{3} =$ ☐
3. $\frac{4}{3} =$ ☐
4. $\frac{7}{3} =$ ☐
5. $\frac{10}{3} =$ ☐
6. $\frac{5}{3} =$ ☐

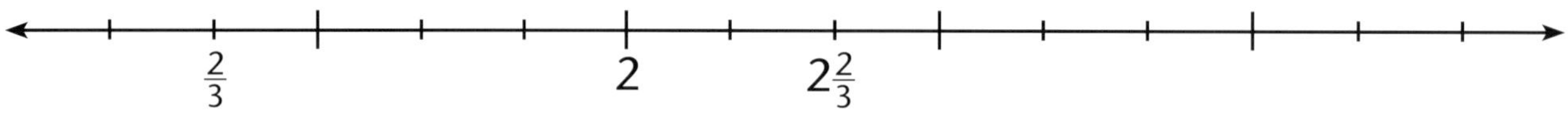

7. $\frac{13}{4} =$ ☐
8. $\frac{7}{4} =$ ☐
9. $\frac{8}{4} =$ ☐
10. $\frac{14}{4} =$ ☐
11. $\frac{4}{4} =$ ☐
12. $\frac{10}{4} =$ ☐
13. $\frac{15}{4} =$ ☐
14. $\frac{5}{4} =$ ☐
15. $\frac{12}{4} =$ ☐

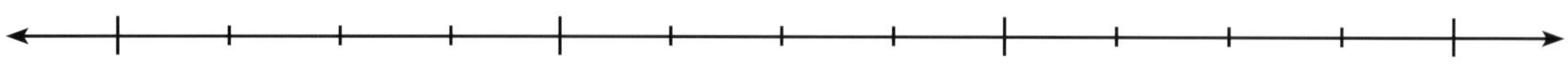

16. $\frac{2}{5} =$ ☐
17. $\frac{10}{5} =$ ☐
18. $\frac{18}{5} =$ ☐
19. $\frac{13}{5} =$ ☐
20. $\frac{20}{5} =$ ☐
21. $\frac{15}{5} =$ ☐
22. $\frac{17}{5} =$ ☐
23. $\frac{6}{5} =$ ☐
24. $\frac{14}{5} =$ ☐
25. $\frac{9}{5} =$ ☐

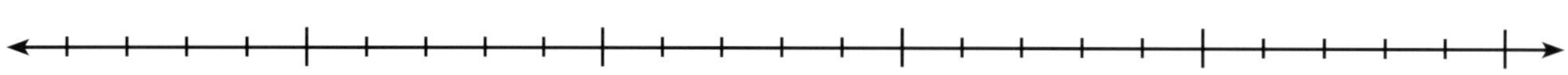

26. $\frac{25}{10} =$ ☐
27. $\frac{37}{10} =$ ☐
28. $\frac{30}{10} =$ ☐
29. $\frac{26}{10} =$ ☐
30. $\frac{20}{10} =$ ☐
31. $\frac{31}{10} =$ ☐
32. $\frac{35}{10} =$ ☐
33. $\frac{40}{10} =$ ☐

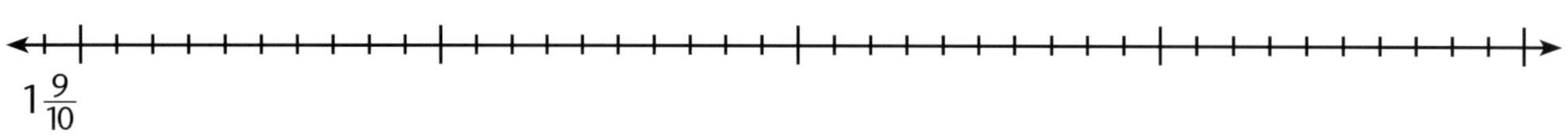

Creating equivalent ratios

I am learning to create equivalent ratios by repeated copying.

For every four apples the monkey eats, she also eats three bananas.

A. How many apples does the monkey eat if she eats...

1. 9 bananas? ______ apples
2. 21 bananas? ______ apples
3. 15 bananas? ______ apples

B. How many bananas does the monkey eat if she eats...

1. 8 apples? ______ bananas
2. 40 apples? ______ bananas
3. 24 apples? ______ bananas

For every five bags of carrots the elephant eats, she also eats four bales of hay.

C. How many bags of carrots does the elephant eat if she eats...

1. 16 bales of hay? ______ bags of carrots
2. 32 bales of hay? ______ bags of carrots
3. 44 bales of hay? ______ bags of carrots

D. How many bales of hay does the elephant eat if she eats...

1. 25 bags of carrots? ______ bales of hay
2. 40 bags of carrots? ______ bales of hay
3. 15 bags of carrots? ______ bales of hay

For every six grubs the blackbirds eat they also eat eight worms.

E. How many grubs do the blackbirds eat if they eat...

1. 16 worms? ______ grubs
2. 32 worms? ______ grubs
3. 40 worms? ______ grubs

I am learning to create equivalent ratios by repeated copying.

A. Find the equivalent ratios. The first one is started for you.

1. 3 : 4 so ____ : 20 (× 5, × 5)
2. 6 : 2 so ____ : 6
3. 2 : 7 so ____ : 21
4. 4 : 5 so 24 : ____
5. 3 : 5 so 27 : ____
6. 4 : 9 so 16 : ____
7. 3 : 7 so 9 : ____ so ____ : 70
8. ____ : 8 so 16 : 32 so 8 : ____
9. 3 : ____ so ____ : 6 so 36 : 24
10. 60 : 48 so ____ : 4 so 20 : ____

B. For every 2 bags of carrots the elephant eats, he also eats 3 bales of hay. Solve these problems.

How many bales of hay does the elephant eat if he eats...

1. 6 bags of carrots? ____
2. 10 bags of carrots? ____

How may bags of carrots does the elephant eat if he eats...

3. 12 bales of hay? ____
4. 21 bales of hay? ____

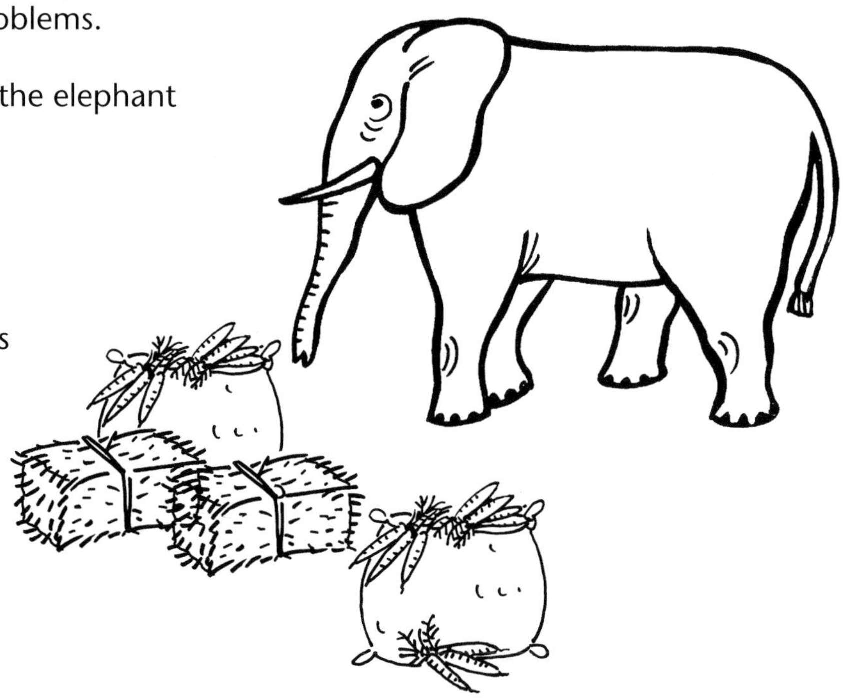

Activity cards

Overview of cards

Fraction rummy

To **make**:

- copy the cards on page 50 and 51 onto coloured paper
- laminate and cut the cards
- store in ziplock bags.

To **play** (with up to four players):

- the dealer shuffles all the cards and deals four to each player
- the dealer places all but one of the remaining cards face down in a pile and puts one "discard card" face up next to the pile
- the dealer starts and picks up either the discard card or the top card from the pile then discards one card from hand
- the game continues in a clockwise direction
- the first player to collect a "family" of fractions is the winner.

Alternative games to play with these cards are:

happy families

snap

fish

memory

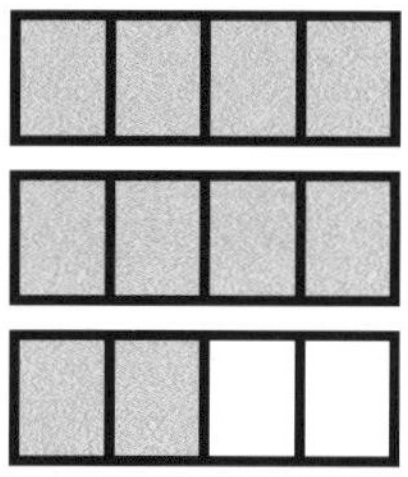	$\frac{10}{4}$	$2\frac{1}{2}$	$2\frac{2}{4}$
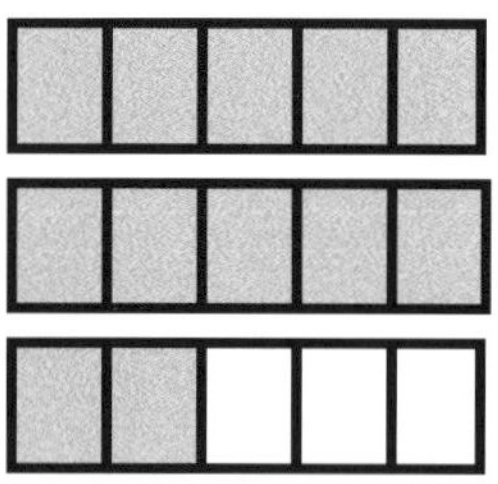	$\frac{12}{5}$	2	$2\frac{4}{10}$
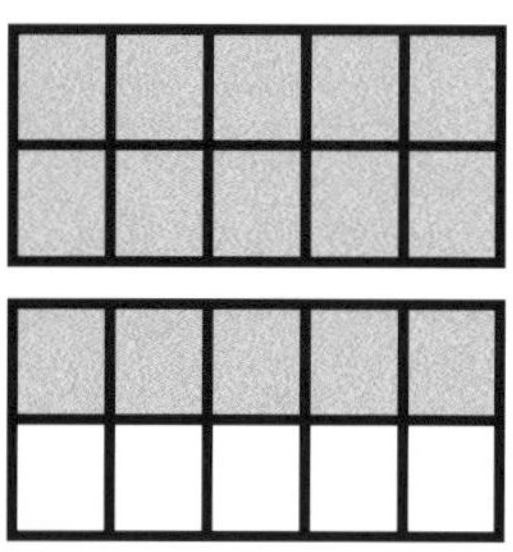	$1\frac{1}{2}$	$1\frac{5}{10}$	$\frac{15}{10}$
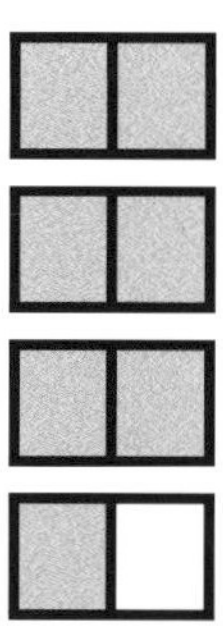	$\frac{7}{2}$	$3\frac{2}{4}$	$3\frac{1}{2}$
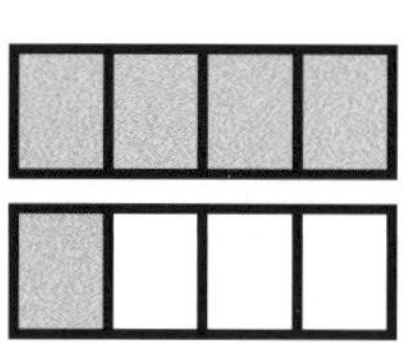	$\frac{5}{4}$	$1\frac{2}{8}$	$1\frac{1}{4}$

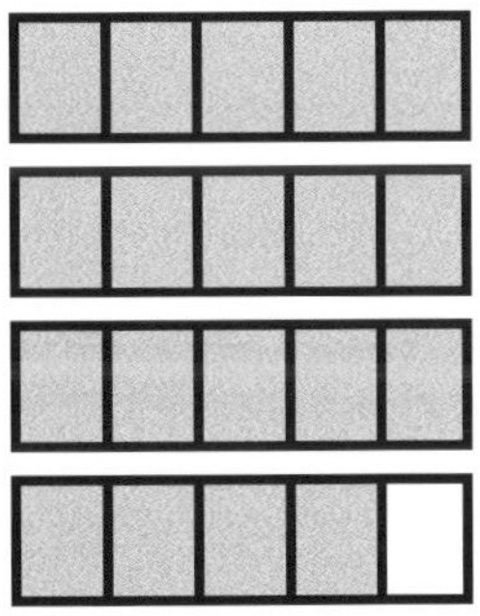	$3\frac{4}{5}$	$\frac{19}{5}$	$3\frac{8}{10}$
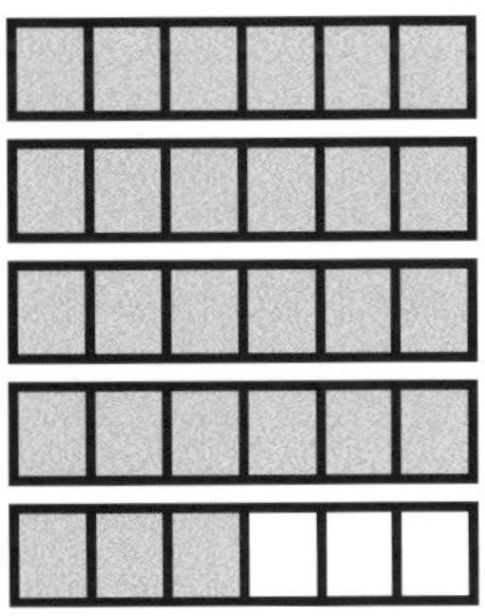	$4\frac{1}{2}$	$4\frac{3}{6}$	$\frac{9}{2}$
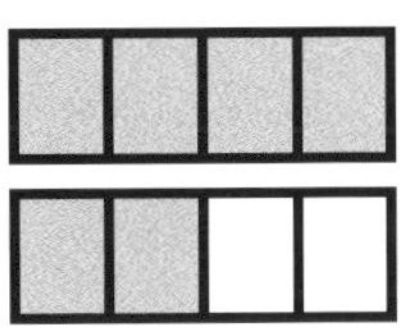	$\frac{2}{4}$	$1\frac{1}{2}$	$\frac{3}{2}$
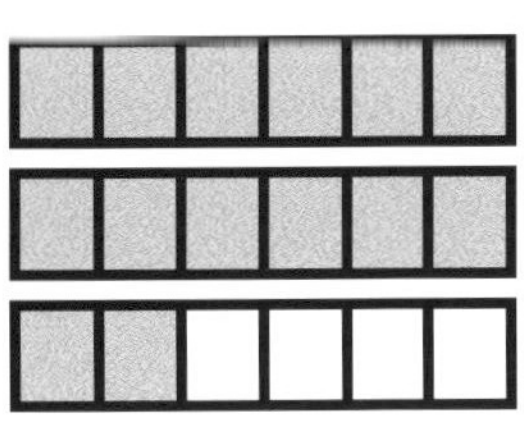	$2\frac{2}{6}$	$2\frac{1}{3}$	$\frac{7}{3}$
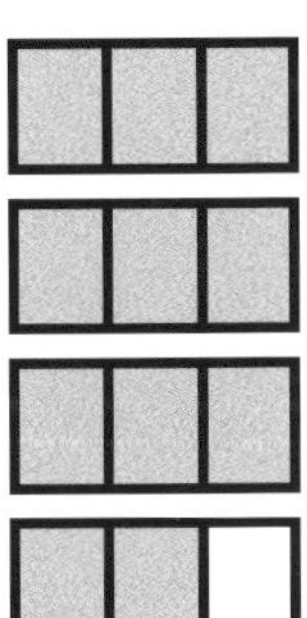	$\frac{11}{3}$	$3\frac{2}{3}$	$3\frac{4}{6}$

Answers to activity sheets

Page 5

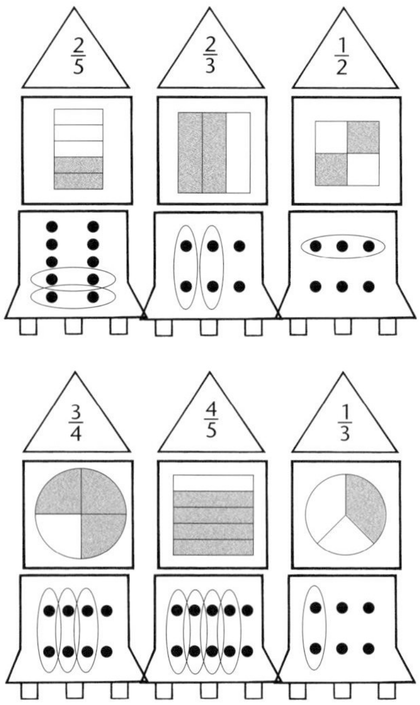

Page 6

A1.	$\frac{2}{5}$	3.	$\frac{3}{4}$	5.	$\frac{4}{5}$
2.	$\frac{3}{4}$	4.	$\frac{2}{3}$	6.	$\frac{2}{3}$

Page 7

A1.	9	B1.	7	C1.	8	D1.	4
2.	27	2.	14	2.	40	2.	16
		3.	35				

Page 8

1.	$1\frac{1}{2}$	5.	4	9.	$1\frac{1}{2}$
2.	$2\frac{2}{3}$	6.	2	10.	2
3.	$1\frac{2}{5}$	7.	$1\frac{2}{8}$	11.	$1\frac{1}{10}$
4.	$1\frac{1}{8}$	8.	$1\frac{4}{5}$	12.	3

Page 10 Final answers

1. $\frac{1}{2}$ of 8 = 4
2. $\frac{1}{2}$ of 18 = 9
3. $\frac{1}{2}$ of 14 = 7
4. $\frac{1}{2}$ of 20 = 10
5. $\frac{1}{2}$ of 4 = 2
6. $\frac{1}{2}$ of 12 = 6

Page 10 continued

7. $\frac{1}{2}$ of 22 = 11
8. $\frac{1}{2}$ of 6 = 3
9. $\frac{1}{2}$ of 10 = 5
10. $\frac{1}{2}$ of 16 = 8

Page 11 Final answers

1.	3	3.	2	5.	8
2.	4	4.	5		

Page 12 Final answers

1.	2	3.	3	5.	6
2.	4	4.	12		

Page 13 Final answers

1. $\frac{1}{3}$ of 18 = 6
2. $\frac{1}{4}$ of 36 = 9
3. $\frac{1}{3}$ of 30 = 10
4. $\frac{1}{5}$ of 30 = 6
5. $\frac{1}{5}$ of 25 = 5
6. $\frac{1}{3}$ of 36 = 12
7. $\frac{1}{4}$ of 400 = 100
8. $\frac{1}{4}$ of 80 = 20
9. $\frac{1}{10}$ of 80 = 8
10. $\frac{1}{8}$ of 400 = 50
11. $\frac{1}{8}$ of 16 = 2
12. $\frac{1}{10}$ of 30 = 3

Page 14 Final answers

1. $\frac{1}{3}$ of 12 = 4
2. $\frac{2}{3}$ of 12 = 8
3. $\frac{3}{3}$ of 12 = 12
4. $\frac{1}{3}$ of 15 = 5
5. $\frac{2}{3}$ of 15 = 10
6. $\frac{3}{3}$ of 15 = 15
7. $\frac{1}{4}$ of 16 = 4
8. $\frac{2}{4}$ of 16 = 8
9. $\frac{3}{4}$ of 16 = 12

Page 14 continued

10. $\frac{4}{4}$ of 16 = 16
11. $\frac{1}{4}$ of 8 = 2
12. $\frac{2}{4}$ of 8 = 4
13. $\frac{3}{4}$ of 8 = 6
14. $\frac{4}{4}$ of 8 = 8
15. $\frac{1}{4}$ of 12 = 3
16. $\frac{2}{4}$ of 12 = 6
17. $\frac{3}{4}$ of 12 = 9
18. $\frac{4}{4}$ of 12 = 12
19. $\frac{1}{5}$ of 20 = 4
20. $\frac{2}{5}$ of 20 = 8
21. $\frac{3}{5}$ of 20 = 12
22. $\frac{4}{5}$ of 20 = 16
23. $\frac{5}{5}$ of 20 = 20

Page 15

1. 5 + 5 = 10
2. 7 + 7 + 7 = 21
3. 3 + 3 + 3 = 9
4. 6 + 6 + 6 = 18
5. 10 + 10 + 10 + 10 = 40
6. 4 + 4 + 4 = 12
7. 4 + 4 + 4 + 4 + 4 + 4 + 4 + 4 + 4 = 36
8. 12 + 12 = 24
9. 10 + 10 + 10 + 10 + 10 + 10 + 10 = 70
10. 8 + 8 + 8 + 8 + 8 = 40

Page 16 Answers may vary.

1. 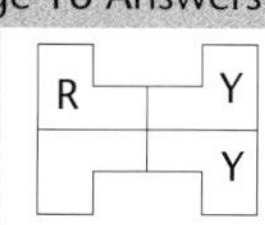

2. 

3. 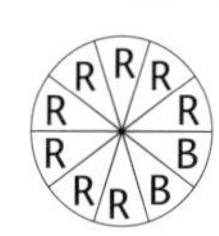

4. 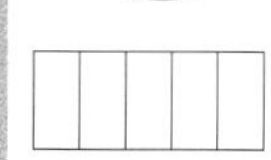

5. 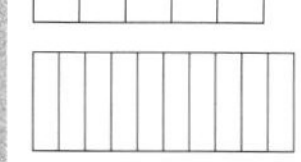

6. 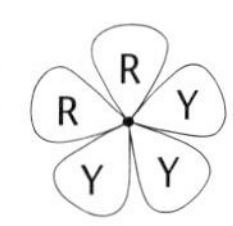

7. 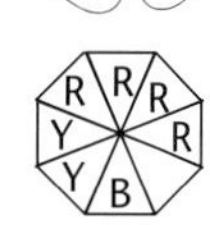

8. 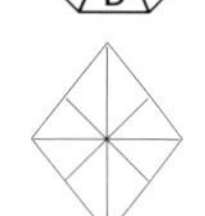

9. 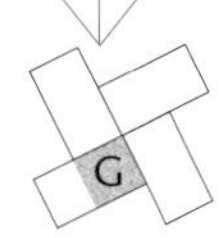

Page 17

A1.	$\frac{1}{8}$ $\frac{1}{4}$ $\frac{1}{2}$	5.	$\frac{1}{5}$ $\frac{1}{4}$ $\frac{1}{2}$	9.	$\frac{1}{8}$ $\frac{1}{5}$ $\frac{1}{2}$
2.	$\frac{1}{4}$ $\frac{1}{3}$ $\frac{1}{2}$	6.	$\frac{1}{9}$ $\frac{1}{6}$ $\frac{1}{3}$	10.	$\frac{1}{5}$ $\frac{1}{4}$ $\frac{1}{3}$
3.	$\frac{1}{10}$ $\frac{1}{8}$ $\frac{1}{5}$	7.	$\frac{1}{12}$ $\frac{1}{8}$ $\frac{1}{2}$		
4.	$\frac{1}{10}$ $\frac{1}{8}$ $\frac{1}{3}$	8.	$\frac{1}{8}$ $\frac{1}{5}$ $\frac{1}{3}$		

Page 18

A2.	seventeen eighths, $2\frac{1}{8}$
3.	$\frac{23}{10}$, $2\frac{3}{10}$
4.	$\frac{8}{3}$, $2\frac{2}{3}$
5.	six quarters, $1\frac{2}{4}$ or $1\frac{1}{2}$
6.	seven halves, $\frac{7}{2}$
7.	$\frac{12}{5}$, $2\frac{2}{5}$
8.	$\frac{9}{4}$, $2\frac{1}{4}$
9.	fifteen tenths, $1\frac{5}{10}$ or $1\frac{1}{2}$
10.	$\frac{9}{8}$, $1\frac{1}{8}$
11.	nine ninths, 1
12.	sixteen fifths, $\frac{16}{5}$
B.	Kerry, Kate, Shay and Isabella, Mary, Joseph, Tom, Christine, Jaeden, Michael, Neve, Shannon

Page 19

1.	Theo, Tom, Tim
2.	Wendy, Wilber, Wilamena, Winston
3.	Sonia, Samuel, Suzi, Sally, Simon

Page 20 Answers may vary

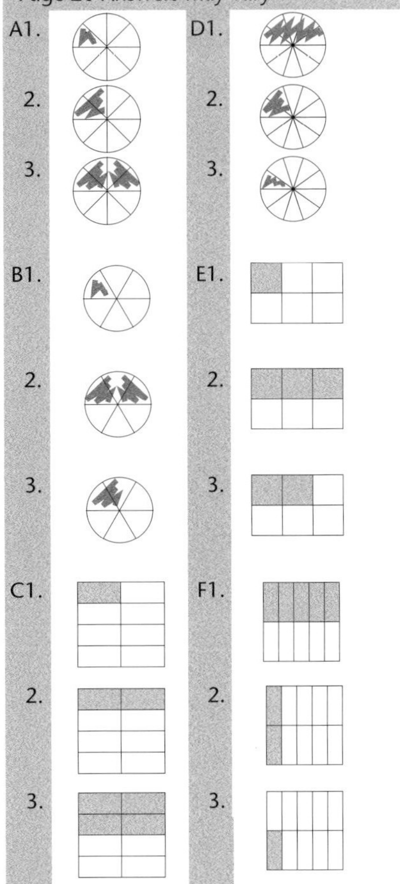

G.	R B B G G G G
H.	R R B B B B B G

Page 21

A2.	8.354	6.	3.123
3.	2.266	7.	1.421
4.	9.199	8.	7.389
5.	4.865	9.	0.032

B1.	fourteen point three eight two
2.	six point four one two
3.	eight point five nine three
4.	thirty-six point one five nine
5.	four point six two eight
6.	three point two five eight
7.	eight point nine four seven
8.	five point one zero nine
9.	seven point nine four two
10.	six point eight five four
11.	nine point zero two one
12.	seventy-two point zero three six
13.	eighty-one point one zero five
14.	sixty-two point three zero four

Page 22

A1.	six point three two nine
2.	eight point zero six eight
3.	two point four five nine
4.	seven point two zero eight
5.	nine point five one eight
B1.	eighty-three point six nine eight
2.	five point two six seven
3.	fourteen point two five one
4.	six point zero two five
5.	thirty-seven point zero zero three
6.	ninety point zero one seven

Page 23

1.	67	11.	29	21.	72
2.	35	12.	54	22.	308
3.	24	13.	63	23.	836
4.	63	14.	90	24.	42
5.	26	15.	65	25.	97
6.	73	16.	25	26.	665
7.	29	17.	48	27.	61
8.	18	18.	133	28.	8
9.	56	19.	60	29.	68
10.	35	20.	46	30.	13

Page 24

1.	266	11.	98	21.	510
2.	22	12.	9	22.	46
3.	50	13.	541	23.	19
4.	73	14.	100	24.	78
5.	93	15.	13	25.	40
6.	752	16.	87	26.	47
7.	28	17.	380	27.	48
8.	382	18.	410	28.	369
9.	79	19.	13	29.	54
10.	60	20.	27	30.	155

Page 25

A1.	b	B.	$\frac{1}{2}$, $\frac{1}{3}$, $\frac{1}{4}$, $\frac{1}{5}$, $\frac{1}{10}$
2.	c	C1.	Julia
3.	e	2.	Ravi
4.	d	3.	Latoya
5.	a	4.	Simon
		5.	Neave
		6.	Wil

Page 26 Particular segments marked and coloured may vary

1. 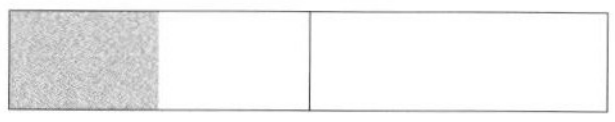

2. 

3. 

4. 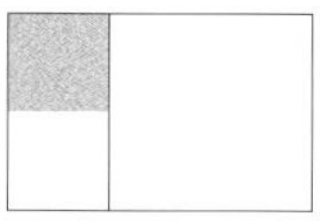

5. 

6. 

7. 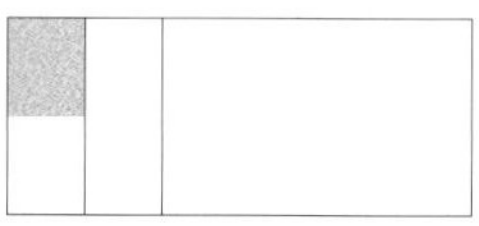

8. 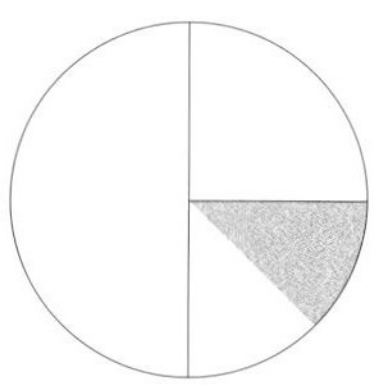

9. 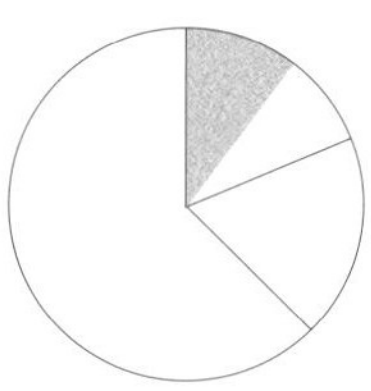

10. 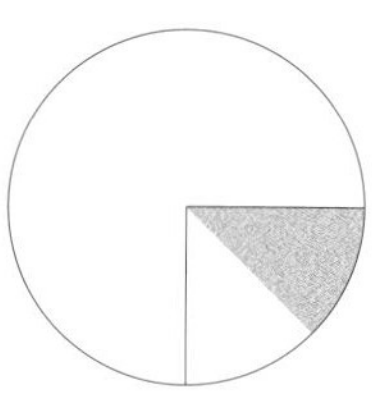

Page 27

1. 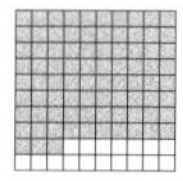 83 hundredths

2. 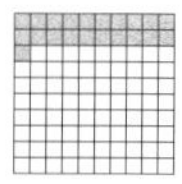 21 hundredths

3.  6 tenths

4.  17 tenths

5. 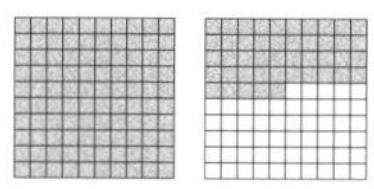 145 hundredths

6. 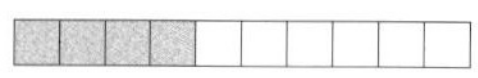 4 tenths

7. 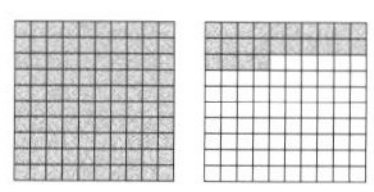 124 hundredths

8. 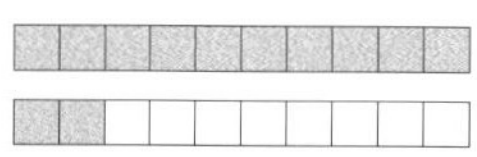 12 tenths

Page 28

1. $2\frac{9}{10}$, 3, $3\frac{1}{10}$, $3\frac{2}{10}$, $3\frac{3}{10}$, $3\frac{4}{10}$, $3\frac{5}{10}$
2. 4, $4\frac{1}{2}$, 5, $5\frac{1}{2}$, 6, $6\frac{1}{2}$, 7
3. $8\frac{2}{4}$, $8\frac{3}{4}$, 9, $9\frac{1}{4}$, $9\frac{2}{4}$, $9\frac{3}{4}$, 10
4. 1, $1\frac{1}{5}$, $1\frac{2}{5}$, $1\frac{3}{5}$, $1\frac{4}{5}$, 2, $2\frac{1}{5}$
5. 5, $5\frac{1}{3}$, $5\frac{2}{3}$, 6, $6\frac{1}{3}$, $6\frac{2}{3}$, 7

Page 29

1. $\frac{10}{10}$, $\frac{11}{10}$, $\frac{12}{10}$, $\frac{13}{10}$, $\frac{14}{10}$, $\frac{15}{10}$, $\frac{16}{10}$
2. $\frac{2}{2}$, $\frac{3}{2}$, $\frac{4}{2}$, $\frac{5}{2}$, $\frac{6}{2}$, $\frac{7}{2}$, $\frac{8}{2}$
3. $\frac{10}{4}$, $\frac{11}{4}$, $\frac{12}{4}$, $\frac{13}{4}$, $\frac{14}{4}$, $\frac{15}{4}$, $\frac{16}{4}$
4. $\frac{6}{3}$, $\frac{7}{3}$, $\frac{8}{3}$, $\frac{9}{3}$, $\frac{10}{3}$, $\frac{11}{3}$, $\frac{12}{3}$
5. $\frac{4}{5}$, $\frac{5}{5}$, $\frac{6}{5}$, $\frac{7}{5}$, $\frac{8}{5}$, $\frac{9}{5}$, $\frac{10}{5}$

Page 30

1. $\frac{1}{5}$, $\frac{2}{5}$, $\frac{3}{5}$, $\frac{4}{5}$, 1, $1\frac{1}{5}$, $1\frac{2}{5}$
2. $\frac{1}{4}$, $\frac{2}{4}$, $\frac{3}{4}$, 1, $1\frac{1}{4}$, $1\frac{2}{4}$, $1\frac{3}{4}$
3. $\frac{2}{3}$, 1, $1\frac{1}{3}$, $1\frac{2}{3}$, 2, $2\frac{1}{3}$, $2\frac{2}{3}$
4. $\frac{7}{10}$, $\frac{8}{10}$, $\frac{9}{10}$, 1, $1\frac{1}{10}$, $1\frac{2}{10}$, $1\frac{3}{10}$
5. $\frac{1}{2}$, 1, $1\frac{1}{2}$, 2, $2\frac{1}{2}$, 3, $3\frac{1}{2}$

Page 31

A1. 0.1, 0.2, 0.3, 0.4, 0.5, 0.6, 0.7, 0.8, 0.7, 0.6, 0.5, 0.4, 0.3, 0.2, 0.1
2. 7.3, 7.4, 7.5, 7.6, 7.7, 7.8, 7.9, 8.0, 7.9, 7.8, 7.7, 7.6, 7.5, 7.4, 7.3
3. 4.6, 4.7, 4.8, 4.9, 5.0, 5.1, 5.2, 5.3, 5.2, 5.1, 5.0, 4.9, 4.8, 4.7, 4.6
4. 9.4, 9.5, 9.6, 9.7, 9.8, 9.9, 10.0, 10.1, 10.0, 9.9, 9.8, 9.7, 9.6, 9.5 9.4

Page 32

A1. 8.63, 8.64, 8.65, 8.66, 8.67, 8.68, 8.69, 8.70, 8.71, 8.70, 8.69, 8.68, 8.67, 8.66, 8.65, 8.64
2. 6.92, 6.93, 6.94, 6.95, 6.96, 6.97, 6.98, 6.99, 7.00, 6.99, 6.98, 6.97, 6.96, 6.95, 6.94, 6.93
3. 5.46, 5.47, 5.48, 5.49, 5.50, 5.51, 5.52, 5.53, 5.54, 5.53, 5.52, 5.51, 5.50, 5.49, 5.48, 5.47
4. 1.01, 1.02, 1.03, 1.04, 1.05, 1.06, 1.07, 1.08, 1.09, 1.08, 1.07, 1.06, 1.05, 1.04, 1.03, 1.02

Page 33

1.

64.0	64.1	64.2	64.3	64.4	64.5	64.6	64.7	64.8
	64.11				64.51			
	64.12				64.52			
	64.13				64.53			
64.04	64.14	64.24	64.34	64.44	64.54	64.64	64.74	64.84

Page 33

2.

		761.48	761.49	761.50	761.51	761.52
		761.38				
		761.28				
		761.18				
761.06	761.07	761.08	761.09	762		

3.

781.72	781.82	780.92
		780.93
		780.94
		780.95
		780.96
		780.97
		780.98
		780.99
		781

4.

487.34	487.35	487.36	487.37	487.38		
				487.28		
				487.18		
				487.08		
		486.96	486.97	486.98	486.99	487

5.

38.8				38.84
38.7				38.74
38.6				38.64
38.5	38.51	38.52	38.53	38.54
38.4				38.44
38.3				38.34
38.2				38.24
38.1	38.11	38.12	38.13	38.14
38.0				38.04

Page 34

1.	1.3, 1.4, 1.5
2.	2.7, 2.8, 2.9
3.	4.2, 4.3, 4.4
4.	2.1, 2.2, 2.3
5.	3.5, 3.6, 3.7
6.	4.6, 4.7, 4.8
7.	20.5, 20.6, 20.7
8.	21.7, 21.8, 21.9
9.	23.3, 23.4, 23.5
10.	21.3, 21.4, 21.5
11.	22.4, 22.5, 22.6
12.	23.8, 23.9, 24
13.	55.3, 55.4, 55.5
14.	56.6, 56.7, 56.8
15.	58.5, 58.6, 58.7
16.	56.3, 56.4, 56.5
17.	57.6, 57.7, 57.8
18.	59.2, 59.3, 59.4
19.	73.4, 73.5, 73.6
20.	74.5, 74.6, 74.7
21.	76.2, 76.3, 76.4
22.	74.2, 74.3, 74.4
23.	75.3, 75.4, 75.5
24.	76.7, 76.8, 76.9

Page 35

A1.	8.2, 8.3, 8.4	17.	6.6, 6.7, 6.8
2.	3.5, 3.6, 3.7	18.	2.8, 2.9, 3.0
3.	5.8, 5.9, 6.0	19.	4.1, 4.2, 4.3
4.	7.1, 7.2, 7.3	20.	3.6, 3.7, 3.8
5.	7.4, 7.5, 7.6	B1.	4.7
6.	3.9, 4.0, 4.1	2.	7.6
7.	1.2, 1.3, 1.4	3.	3.5
8.	2.5, 2.6, 2.7	4.	4.2
9.	4.7, 4.8, 4.9	5.	8.4
10.	9.4, 9.5, 9.6	6.	1.3
11.	6.2, 6.3, 6.4	7.	8.0
12.	8.4, 8.5, 8.6	8.	2.6
13.	9.5, 9.6, 9.7	9.	2.9
14.	5.1, 5.2, 5.3	10.	8.4
15.	7.3, 7.4, 7.5	11.	3.0
16.	7.9, 8.0, 8.1	12.	9.5

C1. 6.3, 6.4, 6.5, 6.6, 6.7, 6.8, 6.9, 7.0

2. 9.0, 9.1, 9.2, 9.3, 9.4, 9.5, 9.6, 9.7

Page 36

A1.	11.96, 12.06, 12.16	B1.	21.09
2.	57.05, 57.15, 57.25	2.	40.16
3.	39.96, 40.06, 40.16	3.	58.21
4.	83.11, 83.21, 83.31	4.	68.52
5.	96.39, 96.49, 96.59	5.	52.12
6.	21.42, 21.52, 21.62	6.	52.12
7.	13.75, 13.85, 13.95	7.	68.52
8.	49.26, 49.36, 49.46	8.	40.06
9.	86.32, 86.42, 86.52	9.	96.49
10.	30.17, 30.27, 30.37	10.	13.85
11.	26.93, 27.03, 27.13	11.	21.09
12.	68.42, 68.52, 68.62	12.	57.15
13.	94.53, 94.63, 94.73	13.	27.03
14.	58.11, 58.21, 58.31		
15.	52.02, 52.12, 52.22		
16.	94.69, 94.79, 94.89		
17.	12.28, 12.38, 12.48		
18.	59.84, 59.94, 60.04		
19.	51.75, 51.85, 51.95		
20.	20.99, 21.09, 21.19		

C1. 9.50, 9.60, 9.70, 9.80, 9.90, 10.00, 10.10, 10.20

2. 5.61, 5.71, 5.81, 5.91, 6.01, 6.11, 6.21, 6.31

Page 37

A1.	2	13.	10	B1.	48
2.	8	14.	3	2.	20
3.	3	15.	6	3.	27
4.	6	16.	4	4.	30
5.	9	17.	9	5.	32
6.	4	18.	5	6.	45
7.	2	19.	9	7.	30
8.	9	20.	7	8.	36
9.	5	21.	6	C1.	$\frac{1}{10}$
10.	10	22.	8	2.	$\frac{1}{7}$
11.	6	23.	5	3.	$\frac{1}{9}$
12.	3	24.	2	4.	$\frac{1}{4}$

Page 38

A1.	F	A7.	F	B4.	49
2.	T	8.	T	5.	56
3.	T	9.	T	6.	27
4.	F	B1.	10	7.	24
5.	F	2.	6	8.	27
6.	T	3.	32		

Page 39

A1.	$\frac{1}{4}$	6.	$\frac{2}{3}$	4.	$\frac{1}{24}$
2.	$\frac{2}{3}$	7.	$\frac{1}{10}$	5.	$\frac{1}{4}$
3.	$\frac{3}{5}$	B1.	$\frac{1}{2}$	C1.	$\frac{1}{3}$
4.	$\frac{1}{3}$	2.	$\frac{1}{8}$	2.	$\frac{1}{4}$
5.	$\frac{3}{4}$	3.	$\frac{1}{12}$	3.	$\frac{1}{6}$

Page 40

A1.	$1\frac{1}{2}$	B4.	$\frac{3}{4}$	B9.	$1\frac{1}{3}$
2.	$2\frac{1}{2}$	5.	$\frac{3}{4}$	10.	$1\frac{3}{4}$
3.	$1\frac{1}{3}$	6.	$1\frac{1}{3}$	11.	$1\frac{3}{5}$
B2.	$1\frac{1}{5}$	7.	$\frac{3}{4}$	12.	$1\frac{2}{3}$
3.	$1\frac{1}{4}$	8.	$2\frac{1}{4}$	13.	$\frac{2}{3}$

Page 41

1.	24	3.	16
2.	32	4.	20

Page 42

1.	20	4.	12	7.	$6\frac{3}{4}$
2.	16	5.	$1\frac{1}{2}$	8.	$4\frac{3}{4}$
3.	28	6.	$2\frac{1}{2}$		

Page 43

A1.	20	A9.	44	B7.	$7\frac{1}{2}$
2.	16	10.	40	8.	$13\frac{1}{2}$
3.	36	B1.	$4\frac{1}{2}$	9.	$6\frac{1}{2}$
4.	12	2.	6	10.	4
5.	28	3.	8	C1.	2
6.	32	4.	$12\frac{1}{2}$	2.	4
7.	24	5.	18	3.	3
8.	8	6.	9	4.	$3\frac{3}{5}$

Page 44

1.	$\frac{1}{3}, \frac{3}{3}, \frac{5}{3}, \frac{7}{3}, \frac{8}{3}, \frac{9}{3}, \frac{10}{3}, \frac{12}{3}$
2.	$\frac{2}{4}, \frac{4}{4}, \frac{5}{4}, \frac{7}{4}, \frac{9}{4}, \frac{11}{4}, \frac{12}{4}, \frac{13}{4}$
3.	$\frac{4}{5}, \frac{6}{5}, \frac{8}{5}, \frac{10}{5}, \frac{14}{5}, \frac{16}{5}, \frac{17}{5}, \frac{20}{5}$
4.	$\frac{3}{8}, \frac{7}{8}, \frac{11}{8}, \frac{14}{8}, \frac{17}{8}, \frac{20}{8}, \frac{24}{8}, \frac{27}{8}$
5.	$\frac{2}{10}, \frac{8}{10}, \frac{12}{10}, \frac{20}{10}, \frac{25}{10}, \frac{30}{10}, \frac{35}{10}, \frac{39}{10}$

Page 45

2.	$1\frac{2}{5}, 1\frac{2}{5}$	15.	2, 2
3.	$\frac{7}{3}, 2\frac{1}{3}$	16.	$\frac{22}{6}, 3\frac{2}{3}$
4.	$\frac{20}{6}, 3\frac{1}{3}$	17.	$1\frac{3}{5}, 1\frac{3}{5}$
5.	$2\frac{2}{8}, 2\frac{1}{4}$	18.	$3\frac{1}{3}, 3\frac{1}{3}$
6.	$\frac{7}{4}, 1\frac{3}{4}$	19.	$\frac{9}{5}, 1\frac{4}{5}$
7.	$2\frac{3}{5}, 2\frac{3}{5}$	20.	$4\frac{2}{8}, 4\frac{1}{4}$
8.	$2\frac{2}{3}, 2\frac{2}{3}$	21.	$1\frac{1}{3}, 1\frac{1}{3}$
9.	$\frac{12}{5}, 2\frac{2}{5}$	22.	$\frac{16}{5}, 3\frac{1}{5}$
10.	$3\frac{3}{6}, 3\frac{1}{2}$	23.	$3\frac{6}{10}, 3\frac{3}{5}$
11.	$2\frac{1}{4}, 2\frac{1}{4}$	24.	$\frac{14}{4}, 3\frac{1}{2}$
12.	–, $\frac{3}{4}$	25.	$2\frac{4}{5}, 2\frac{4}{5}$
13.	$4\frac{1}{3}, 4\frac{1}{3}$	26.	$\frac{11}{3}, 3\frac{2}{3}$
14.	$\frac{5}{3}, 1\frac{2}{3}$		

Page 46

1.	1	3.	$1\frac{1}{3}$	5.	$3\frac{1}{3}$
2.	$2\frac{2}{3}$	4.	$2\frac{1}{3}$	6.	$1\frac{2}{3}$
	$1, 1\frac{1}{3}, 1\frac{2}{3}, 2\frac{1}{3}, 2\frac{2}{3}, 3\frac{1}{3}$				
7.	$3\frac{1}{4}$	10.	$3\frac{2}{4}$	13.	$3\frac{3}{4}$
8.	$1\frac{3}{4}$	11.	1	14.	$1\frac{1}{4}$
9.	2	12.	$2\frac{2}{4}$	15.	3
	$1, 1\frac{1}{4}, 1\frac{3}{4}, 2, 2\frac{2}{4}, 3, 3\frac{1}{4}, 3\frac{2}{4}, 3\frac{3}{4}$				
16.	$\frac{2}{5}$	20.	4	24.	$2\frac{4}{5}$
17.	2	21.	3	25.	$1\frac{4}{5}$
18.	$3\frac{3}{5}$	22.	$3\frac{2}{5}$		
19.	$2\frac{3}{5}$	23.	$1\frac{1}{5}$		
	$\frac{2}{5}, 1\frac{1}{5}, 1\frac{4}{5}, 2, 2\frac{3}{5}, 2\frac{4}{5}, 3, 3\frac{2}{5}, 3\frac{3}{5}, 4$				
26.	$2\frac{1}{5}$	29.	$2\frac{3}{5}$	32.	$3\frac{1}{2}$
27.	$3\frac{7}{10}$	30.	2	33.	4
28.	3	31.	$3\frac{1}{10}$		
	$2, 2\frac{1}{5}, 2\frac{3}{5}, 3, 3\frac{1}{10}, 3\frac{1}{2}, 3\frac{7}{10}, 4$				

Page 47

A1.	12	B3.	18	D2.	32
2.	28	C1.	20	3.	12
3.	20	2.	40	E1.	12
B1.	6	3.	55	2.	24
2.	30	D1.	20	3.	30

Page 48

A1.	15	6.	36	B1.	9
2.	18	7.	21, 30	2.	15
3.	6	8.	4, 16	3.	8
4.	30	9.	2, 9	4.	14
5.	45	10.	5, 16		